RESPONSIVE GUIDED READING
IN GRADES K–5

Solving Problems in the Teaching of Literacy

Cathy Collins Block, Series Editor

RECENT VOLUMES

Responsive
Guided Reading
in Grades K–5

Simplifying Small-Group Instruction

JENNIFER BERNE
SOPHIE C. DEGENER

THE GUILFORD PRESS
New York   London

© 2010 The Guilford Press
A Division of Guilford Publications, Inc.
72 Spring Street, New York, NY 10012
www.guilford.com

Printed in the United States of America

This book is printed on acid-free paper.

Last digit is print number: 9 8 7 6 5 4 3 2 1

Library of Congress Cataloging-in-Publication Data

Berne, Jennifer.
  Responsive guided reading in grades K–5 : simplifying small-group
instruction / Jennifer Berne, Sophie C. Degener.
      p. cm. — (Solving problems in the teaching of literacy)
  Includes bibliographical references and index.
  ISBN 978-1-60623-703-8 (pbk.) — ISBN 978-1-60623-704-5 (hardcover)
  1. Guided reading. 2. Reading (Elementary)   I. Degener, Sophie.
II. Title.
  LB1050.377.B47 2010
  372.41′62—dc22
                                                            2009051597

About the Authors

Jennifer Berne, PhD, is Associate Professor at National-Louis University, where she is also chair of the Department of Reading and Language Arts. She teaches courses in comprehension, the teaching of writing, and literacy methods. Dr. Berne's publications include work on teacher professional development, the teaching of process writing, and comprehension strategy instruction. She spent 10 years in adult literacy, teaching underprepared college students the strategies needed for reading and writing in higher education. This classroom experience has anchored her interest in contemporary literacy practices and informs her work in pre- and inservice teacher learning. In addition to her work teaching, researching, and writing, Dr. Berne acts as a literacy consultant and professional developer in urban, rural, and suburban school districts working to refresh their literacy curriculum.

Sophie C. Degener, EdD, is Assistant Professor in the Department of Reading and Language Arts at National-Louis University, where she teaches classes in beginning reading, reading research, and literacy methods to undergraduates, master's students, and doctoral students. Her research interests include family literacy and primary literacy instruction, and her numerous conference presentations and publications reflect those interests. Prior to her work as a professor, Dr. Degener taught in the primary grades. It is her work with struggling readers and their families that has motivated her interest in helping educators at every grade level to understand the unique needs of each and every student and to design differentiated instruction that best meets those needs.

Acknowledgments

We call the model that we describe in this book *responsive guided reading*. We do so with the full knowledge that many models of guided reading are absolutely responsive to student needs. This title was never intended to take away from models that have proven successful in many classrooms. In fact, we started teaching about guided reading using the models that we had seen and read about. These included those described by Fountas and Pinnell (1996), Opitz and Ford (2001), and others. We would like to make it clear that we greatly admire the work of these literacy leaders, and that the field and we ourselves owe them a great debt. It has been our experience, however, that our beginning teachers were not able to manage the demands of guided reading as described by these scholars in such a way that they could implement it with any regularity. However, we have seen our beginning teachers struggle to manage the demands of guided reading in such a way that they could implement it with any regularity. In this book, we offer a level of specificity that our beginning teachers seemed to need, that the experienced teachers we spoke with seemed to appreciate, and that literacy coaches were better able to communicate to the teachers with whom they work.

We owe gratitude to our colleagues at National-Louis University, especially Dr. Ann Bates, who helped us think through our initial rough ideas about guided reading. We are also indebted to our students in the Chicago Teaching Fellows program who helped tremendously with the evolution of responsive guided reading into its current form. As these new educators shared the real circumstances of their teaching lives, we understood what was and was not possible for their work with students and did our best to adjust accordingly.

Doctoral students Elizabeth Kearney, Sara Morris, and Ivy Sitkoski each contributed their expertise, time, and enthusiasm by completing a variety of tasks that made our work so much easier.

We were blessed to have reviewers who were both critical and generous and whose feedback helped us focus our ideas more effectively. We thank them as well as the staff at The Guilford Press, in particular our editor, Craig Thomas, who encouraged this book from the first.

Close observation of our own children's literacy education has sharpened our ideals about the possible. For this, we thank Peter, Luke, Justin, and Allyson. We want for all children what we want for them: to be in classrooms where the love of reading is always evident, where students' interests are encouraged, and where students' needs are understood and addressed through thoughtful assessment and differentiated instruction.

Contents

Contents

RESPONSIVE GUIDED READING
IN GRADES K–5

Part I

What Is Responsive Guided Reading?

Chapter 1

Introduction

The ideas contained in this book come out of a real need. We are literacy educators who work with both preservice and experienced teachers. We believe that one of the most important components of the literacy day is the kind of customized, differentiated instruction that goes on in guided reading groups. For many years, we have advocated for classroom structures embedded in the literacy block that privilege this practice, and we have encouraged teachers to learn as much about it as they can. Once literacy instructors read work from Fountas and Pinnell (1996) and others like them they see how much sense this practice makes and are anxious to dive in with their own students. Over and over, though, we see their enthusiasm wane as they are literally plowed under with the demands of text selection, planning, classroom management, and assessment that it appears these groups require. More often than we'd hope, by late in the fall guided reading has ceased to exist or at the very most become an occasional occurrence. We are always disappointed to hear of this or observe in classrooms where we expect to see guided reading and do not, but really, we understand. The experience of Mr. Angelos,* a first-grade teacher with whom we worked, is typical of the stories that teachers tell us and can help illustrate the difficulties of successfully implementing guided reading in real classrooms.

It's October and Mr. Angelos is ready to begin guided reading in his first-grade classroom. He has grouped his students accord-

---

*The names of all teachers and students in this book have been changed to protect their identities.

ing to their performance on a number of reading assessments and is confident that they are with like-performing peers. He has scoured the reading materials available in the school building and at the public library so that he might come up with a number of varied-level books on a similar theme. With plans to start guided reading during his literacy block on Monday, he stays up late Sunday night creating lesson plans for each of his guided reading groups.

Monday morning at 9:00, he calls his first group over. The children sit around the table at the back of the room. Mr. Angelos shows them the book they will be reading. It has a picture of two baby penguins on the front cover, and Mr. Angelos asks the students to predict what the book will be about. The students enthusiastically respond, and several launch into stories about their trips to the aquarium where they saw dozens of penguins. They make predictions and continue to relate personal stories as they do a picture walk through the book. Following the picture walk, Mr. Angelos reminds them of a strategy that they had learned the previous week when they discussed using the word wall to help with unknown words. He talks to the students about this strategy, gives an example or two, and then asks them to begin reading. He leans his ear toward each child, trying to discern their reading, but after doing so with two of the children, sees that 40 minutes has elapsed and stops them.

Though he has only met with one group this day, now it's time to go to music. He realizes he will have to meet with his other groups later in the week and wonders when he will get back to this one. By November, Mr. Angelos has only met with each of his groups a handful of times. In December, he shelves guided reading, with the sincere belief that it takes too much time and effort for what it accomplishes.

Though we admire much of what Mr. Angelos was trying to do, we agree that it seems inelegant and cumbersome. We want teachers to work with kids in guided reading groups because we have read the research and seen the results, yet we want all teachers—those with large and small classes, unruly and calm students, in upper elementary and lower elementary—to be able to accomplish this without unreasonable demands on either the teacher, the students in the guided reading group, or the rest of the students who are often left to manage themselves when the teacher pulls groups.

A look into another classroom, that of Ms. Larson, offers us another way to think about guided reading.

Ms. Larson is sitting with five students at the kidney-shaped table in the corner of her second-grade classroom. Each of the students at Ms. Larson's table has a copy of *A Bargain for Frances* by Russell Hoban in front of them. Ms. Larson has selected this text for this particular group of students because she believes it to be at their high instructional level, too difficult for them to decode independently but not so difficult that they cannot manage it with teacher support. She has selected it independently of the books she has selected for her other students. After reading the first few pages with the students, she asks them to continue to read the text silently to themselves as best they can. She reminds them to use all the strategies that have been discussed in large-group shared reading lessons to help decode. She stands up and kneels down next to Brianna who is to her immediate right. Brianna looks up briefly and then starts to read aloud from page 8.

BRIANNA: (*reading*) "Why do I have to be careful?" said Frances. "Re.... " (*Pauses.*)

MS. LARSON: Keep going, see if that helps.

BRIANNA: Keep going?

MS. LARSON: Read to the end of the sentence to see if the other words might help you to figure out this one.

BRIANNA: " ... the last time?"

MS. LARSON: Now go back, look at that word again and see if the first letter and the rest of the sentence helps you to understand.

BRIANNA: "Remember the last time?"

MS. LARSON: Excellent! Look what you did. You used the first two letters and the rest of the sentence to figure it out. That is a great strategy. See if you might continue to use it as you read. (*Moves along to Robert, Alli, and Justin in turn.*)

Ms. Larson ends this group by reminding each student what strategy she worked on with them and asking them to pay attention to using it over the next few days. After the 15-minute group, these students leave and she calls another group to work with her.

Ms. Larson and her students are engaged in what we refer to as *responsive guided reading*. Though responsive guided reading draws much from the work of Fountas and Pinnell (1996), Dorn, French, and Jones (1998), Opitz and Ford (2001), and Routman (2002), and in this sense resembles the guided reading groups of Mr. Angelos, it also has some clear distinctions. First, Ms. Larson does not spend time previewing the errors that she believes the children might make. Second, she intentionally selects a text that she believes will cause the students to miscue fairly quickly, yet she doesn't belabor the text selection or concern herself with matching the theme of this book to the theme of books she will select for other groups. And third, she focuses on individual errors, believing it crucial that students leave the table with a specific, "customized" strategy she promotes for them to work on as they read across their day.

When Ms. Larson was hired to teach second grade, she knew she wanted to implement guided reading because she was drawn to the idea that students could learn from texts that were at their own instructional level. Her building had a leveled book room and it was clear from conversations with her principal and her other team members that guided reading was encouraged in the building. Her observations of the practice, however, left her feeling daunted and deeply concerned about her ability to manage the time it took to do this well. She felt that she had the ability to select different books for different groups of students, but was worried about her ability to tie these books thematically into one another or to have enough time to thoroughly preview, plan, and reflect upon every group lesson across five or six groups of five students each. Like many other teachers, she was faced with a practical dilemma. Should she do what she felt was the right thing—small, differentiated groups—but was certainly overwhelming for a new teacher, or should she revert to the whole-group instruction that she knew could not be differentiated in the same way?

What Ms. Larson found after much thinking and much talking with others was that there was an alternative to the "either guided reading or whole-group model." Ms. Larson decided to implement a streamlined version of what she had seen her colleagues do, a version that required far less planning and was more ad hoc in nature than what she had seen before. While Ms. Larson may ultimately strive to incorporate more of the practices typical of guided reading, it is her belief, and one that we share, that doing something simply and effectively sets one up for long-term innovation and success.

A distinction between traditional static reading groups, guided reading as it is most often practiced, and what we refer to as *responsive* guided reading groups can be seen in Table 1.1. Responsive guided reading relies upon the following principles:

TABLE 1.1. Three Different Approaches to Grouped Reading Instruction

	Texts	Membership	Emphasis	Time per group
Traditional reading groups	Instructional	Static	Skills	Varied
Guided reading groups	Instructional	Dynamic	Strategies	20+ minutes
Responsive reading groups	"High" instructional	Dynamic	Individual take-away strategy	15–20 minutes

1. Responsive guided reading groups have a predictable, transparent structure.
2. In a responsive guided reading group, the teacher waits for the student to miscue before deciding what to teach. Thus, the preplanning is limited.
3. The books chosen for responsive guided reading need not be thematically connected.
4. Responsive guided reading groups are designed to force students to miscue while they have a supportive person with them; thus the texts must be difficult enough to force an error in a short amount of time.
5. Responsive guided reading groups should be brief (15–20 minutes per group).
6. Teaching that can be effectively done with the whole class is not the focus of responsive guided reading groups; rather instruction is limited to that which can only be done in this context.

1. *Responsive guided reading groups have a predictable, transparent structure.* We don't think it is necessary for teachers to spend much time planning their guided reading groups, and we have found that providing a set structure for organizing time during guided reading is something that provides much relief to teachers and students. We have a structure for guided reading that is easy to remember and easy to follow. Each participant in a responsive guided reading group knows exactly what to expect during that time.

Essentially the structure that we offer is one where there is very little preteaching of material. During the first minute, the teacher introduces the book and reminds students of a strategy they've been working on in shared reading which may help them with this book. During the next minute or so, the teacher reads aloud from the book, and then asks students to choral read with him or her. The bulk of the guided reading group is the next 10 minutes when the teacher listens to each child read (2 minutes per child) and provides support to students when they miscue or display evidence of breakdown in their comprehension. The guided reading group concludes with everyone coming back together and reviewing the strategies that each of them tried during their individual reading.

This entire process takes between 15 and 20 minutes. The briefness of the group allows a teacher to easily meet with two groups per day, without unduly taxing the rest of her class's ability to remain engaged in meaningful literacy activities.

2. *In a responsive guided reading group, the teacher waits for the student to miscue or display evidence of a comprehension breakdown before deciding what to teach. Thus, the preplanning is limited.* In a responsive guided reading group, student needs are what dictate the curriculum. It is the reading of the student that tells the teacher what the student can learn in that moment. Consider the following. Stephanie is a fourth-grade student; her teacher is listening to her read a passage out of a *National Geographic Kids* article titled "Amazing Pet Rescue" (Lynda D. Jones, June–July 2008, p. 32). The text reads, "On any given day there's a menagerie of cats, dogs, reptiles, or birds hanging out at Shapiro's sanctuary, waiting to be adopted." Stephanie reads, "On any given day there's a man-a, man-a," and stops. Her teacher, Ms. Lopez-Johnson, waits for a moment as Stephanie struggles and watches her as she attempts to use her knowledge to figure out the unknown word. When it is clear that Stephanie's independent strategies will not help her decode and/ or understand that unknown word, her teacher offers her a prompt. Ms. Lopez-Johnson suggests that Stephanie read just the first part of the word and then use the rest of the sentence to approximate the meaning. Though Stephanie never decodes the word accurately, she does, with some coaching from her teacher, make a reasonable inference that the word means "lots of." Ms. Lopez-Johnson talks to her about using what she knows about the other words to infer the meaning of this one and encourages her to do so as she continues to read. Ms. Lopez-Johnson did not plan to work on that word or that strategy in particular; instead, she let Stephanie's reading tell her what her needs were.

The next student may very well read a different page to Ms. Lopez-Johnson and she might cue him on a different word in a different way. It is likely that most of the students would struggle with the word *menag-*

erie and that it was only Stephanie who worked on that word. Other students worked on other words and this is just fine as Ms. Lopez-Johnson's goal is not to teach about any one word in particular, but rather to build the students' repertoire of strategies to use when they come to any unknown word as they read in varied contexts.

3. *The books chosen for responsive guided reading need not be thematically connected or integrated into the rest of the curriculum.* One of the largest drains on teacher time and energy is attempting to thematically link guided reading books across performance levels. If teachers believe that they have to come up with five books, at different levels, all on the same topic, they might find themselves spending all their time in the book room pulling texts or online locating reading materials. In responsive guided reading, the goal is learning how to read beyond the text at hand, thus the text becomes a tool for learning a new strategy. In this respect, the actual content is not as crucial as the strategies learned. There are many times in the literacy day when content is very, very important, when we try to use reading to engage students with literature or other content-area curriculum. We would never say that content is not important in teaching a child to read better, but rather that in a context like responsive guided reading we aren't nearly as worried about it.

4. *Responsive guided reading groups are designed to force students to miscue or display evidence of a comprehension breakdown while they have a supportive person with them; thus the texts must be difficult enough to force an error in a short amount of time.* Most teachers are familiar with the notion of independent-, instructional-, and frustration-level texts. An independent-level book is one that a child can read easily and comfortably such that explicit instruction in strategy use is not required for good comprehension. Typically, a teacher can determine if a book is at a child's independent level if that child can read the book with 96–100% accuracy. An instructional-level book is one with which students can make some meaning with teacher support. A book is at a child's instructional level if the child can read it with 90–95% accuracy. This is the place where literacy educators (e.g., Dorn, French, & Jones, 1998; Fountas & Pinnell, 1996) believe students have the most opportunity to learn. Because the text challenges are just beyond their grasp, the support of a teacher or other skillful reader may be enough to help the child make meaning. The hope is that this immediate instruction will be transferable so that when the child encounters a similar text challenge when reading independently, he or she will employ the strategy, thus propelling him or her to new reading capabilities. A frustration-level

text (one that a child reads with less than 90% accuracy) is one that is far beyond a child's capabilities and will likely agitate him or her even with support. Teachers should refrain from asking a child to learn from something that is clearly beyond his or her current abilities.

In responsive guided reading groups, teachers should plan to use texts that they believe will cause students to miscue or display a breakdown of strategy use fairly quickly, within the first few moments of reading for primary readers and within a minute or two for upper-grade readers. If the child goes on too long without struggle, the teacher has lost the opportunity for assisting, as he or she will need to get on to the next student. We call the level of texts that is ideal for use in a responsive guided reading group "high instructional." (See above and below for discussion of time frames for responsive guided reading groups.)

Many teachers remind children that the purpose of the responsive guided reading group is to force errors; they tell them not to be ashamed or worried if they struggle because the book was chosen so that they will. Though this is an odd concept for students, repetition of it will surely smooth out some of their discomfort.

It is counterintuitive to wish students to fail at a task. So much of a teacher's job is to help students have success. In a responsive guided reading group, teachers are able to customize their instruction because students miscue or otherwise demonstrate inappropriate strategy use as they read. Without this breakdown, the teacher is left only to encourage children to keep reading. When a teacher notes that a child does not struggle with a text as the other group members do, it is worth considering moving the child to another group. Similarly, if a child struggles more than the other group members, it may indicate that the text is at his or her frustration level, not an appropriate text level for reasonable instruction in a responsive guided reading group.

5. *Responsive guided reading groups should be brief (15–20 minutes per group).* One of the most dramatic differences between responsive guided reading groups and other kinds of guided reading groups is that they are purposefully brief. One reason is that we designed them for teachers just getting their feet wet in this kind of instruction. Most teachers, even brand-new to the field, can help the rest of the class work quietly on independent, group, or paired work for short amounts of time. The engagement of other students in meaningful work while the teacher is working with a small group is so crucial. It seemed unrealistic to believe that this might be done for more than short amounts of time. Generally, teachers who use the model we are describing see two groups per day. Thus, the remaining students are asked to behave and

work well together or independently (or both depending on the preference of the teacher, the grade, and the context) for up to 20 minutes in two different sessions: first, as the teacher works with the first group and then after a 5-minute break and possible redirection of the remainder of the class, as the teacher works with the second group. Please see the section above for the timing of the actual activities as they are done in the responsive reading groups.

6. *Teaching that can be effectively done with the whole class is not the focus of responsive guided reading groups; rather instruction is limited to that which can only be done in this context.* Any lesson that can be done as a shared reading, whole-group lesson is not typically part of responsive guided reading groups. The value of placing students in guided reading groups is that the teacher has the ability to listen to them read alone, an activity that cannot be done in a whole group. Because this is such a crucial endeavor in helping kids to read better, any activities that take away from that time should be moved into the large group context or another teaching mode. For example, Ms. Larson sees that her most capable reading group could benefit from asking questions about the text as they read to themselves, in order to improve their comprehension. However, to teach this strategy well, she would need to explain and model using the questioning strategy, something that would take up the entire time (or more) allotted for this group. Far more effective would be to teach questioning during a shared reading time with her whole class. In that way, each of her students, regardless of their reading capabilities, would be exposed to an important comprehension strategy, and each of them would see how a competent reader (Ms. Larson) uses that strategy. After modeling questioning with the whole group and having students practice asking questions about texts during shared reading, Ms. Larson could then refer to this strategy while working with a guided reading group. She might say:

> "While I was reading *James and the Giant Peach* [by Roald Dahl] to the whole class yesterday, you practiced thinking about the questions you had as I read. When you ask questions while you read, it helps you to better understand what you know and what you still need to find out. Today while you read, I want you to write down the questions that you have on a Post-it note and then stick the Post-it in the spot where the question came up."

In this way, Ms. Larson is asking students to begin utilizing, individually, a strategy they learned with the whole group. She still has plenty of time to listen to students read aloud and provide support for their reading.

The success of this model relies upon the cueing of the teacher as she works with individual students. It is our belief that having a predictable structure allows the teacher to focus on this very important component. The question remains: How do we help teachers better understand the process of providing instantaneous support and scaffolding to their students during guided reading groups? Picard (2005) speaks to this issue as she describes her collaboration with a master teacher who provided coaching and support for a full school year. Picard spent hours observing this teacher doing guided reading, which allowed her to learn the vocabulary of the prompts this teacher provided students to help them in their reading. Picard was also shadowed by this teacher during her own work with guided reading groups and got feedback about her scaffolding attempts. Picard describes this process as invaluable in learning how to best support her students' progress in reading.

Indeed, it is a coaching model such as this that we believe is most effective in helping the teachers that we work with to become more comfortable in providing instantaneous and targeted scaffolding to more effectively impact the reading progress of each individual student. Short of this, we have offered suggestions based on many years of working with students in groups and watching expert and new teachers manage the groups. We hope that this will be a start for teachers new to this kind of instruction.

We haven't solved all the issues related to helping teachers run effective guided reading groups. Much work remains. In addition, much research looking carefully at the effect of this practice on student learning will be most welcome. What we have done is streamlined the process of guided reading by recasting it as responsive guided reading, a practice that we believe to be effective, efficient, and realistic. While the model we propose limits time in guided reading groups to about 15–20 minutes per group, it is important to be clear that the overall time students read is actually increased. A discussion of the place responsive guided reading holds in the entire literacy block can be found in Chapter 2.

We have organized the book into three parts. The first two parts give a detailed description of responsive guided reading: what it is and how it fits into the balanced literacy classroom, as well as a closeup look at how the teacher scaffolds student reading during primary and intermediate responsive guided reading groups. The third part was written to address those aspects of guided reading that teachers we've worked with have identified as barriers to guided reading instruction, including a thorough look at how to get started with guided reading at the beginning of each school year. A more detailed look at the three parts follows.

• *Part 1: What Is Responsive Guided Reading?* Chapter 1 introduces responsive guided reading and explains how it is informed by and differs from other models of guided reading instruction. Chapter 2 is a discussion of balanced literacy instruction and how the responsive guided reading fits into a balanced literacy block. Chapter 3 is a detailed guide to the work the teacher does in the responsive guided reading group: what he or she says, how long it takes, how the process evolves.

• *Part II: Teacher Cueing in Responsive Guided Reading Groups.* Chapter 4 looks at responsive guided reading in the primary grades and the kinds of cues teachers can provide to beginning readers as they struggle to decode unknown words. Chapter 5 looks at responsive guided reading in the upper elementary grades and the kinds of cues teachers can provide to their more fluent readers who need teacher support using comprehension and vocabulary strategies.

• *Part III: Getting Started with Responsive Guided Reading: Practical Considerations.* Chapter 6 provides guidance in teaching students to function independently while others are in groups. We emphasize the importance of systematically establishing routines for independent literacy activities prior to getting started with responsive guided reading. Chapter 7 explores worthwhile and manageable independent literacy activities for students who are not working with the teacher during guided reading time. Chapter 8 is about assessing students' literacy abilities and attitudes and using that information to place them in responsive guided reading groups. Chapter 9 shows teachers how to revisit grouping decisions throughout the course of the school year, and how to approach the valuable idea of flexible grouping. Chapter 10 guides teachers on selecting materials for responsive guided reading groups.

RESOURCES FOR FURTHER READING

Booth D. W. (2000). *Guiding the reading process: Techniques and strategies for successful instruction in K–8.* York, ME: Stenhouse/Pembroke.

This is a compilation of dozens of brief explanations of reading practices and strategies, from ideas on how to develop phonics strategies to how to conduct genre and author studies. Many of the ideas work well within a classroom in which guided reading is the focus.

Cunningham, P. M., Hall, D. P., & Cunningham, J. W. (2000). *Guided reading the four blocks way*. Greensboro, NC: Carson-Dellosa.

This book explains guided reading as one of the blocks in the *four-block* framework. Much of the book focuses on teaching comprehension during guided reading with strategies such as KWL charts, graphic organizers, and discussion. The remainder deals with effective formats to use during guided reading such as choral reading, shared reading, and book club groups.

Diller, D. (2007). *Making the most of small groups: Differentiation for all*. York, ME: Stenhouse.

This book focuses on the teacher's role during small-group instruction. After discussing basics such as time, organization, and grouping, the author devotes a chapter to each essential reading element: comprehension, fluency, phonemic awareness, phonics, and vocabulary. She presents numerous practical applications in each area by offering teacher promptings, possible lesson focuses, and even detailed lesson plans.

Ford, M. P., & Opitz, M. F. (2008). Guided reading: Then and now. In M. J. Fresch (Ed.), *An essential history of current reading practices* (pp. 66–81). Newark, DE: International Reading Association.

This selection provides a brief history of guided reading as well as the authors' definition, viewpoints on it, and thoughts for the future. It provides 11 common understandings of guided reading that have withstood the test of time.

Fountas, I. C., & Pinnell, G. S. (1996). *Guided reading: Good first teaching for all children*. Portsmouth, NH. Heinemann.

The authors explain how guided reading is the answer to building a literate community that meets the needs of individual readers. They communicate how to create an effective balanced literacy program based on guided reading, and supported by read-aloud, shared reading, interactive writing, and other approaches. Included are guidelines for observation and assessment, dynamic grouping of readers, and more. The appendices include well over 2,500 leveled books and reproducibles for organization, instruction, and record keeping.

Opitz, M. F., & Ford, M. P. (2001). *Reaching readers: Flexible and innovative strategies for guided reading*. Portsmouth, NH: Heinemann.

The authors call their model a "second-generation" model of guided reading, one that challenges educators to expand their vision and experiment with alternative practices. The reader will find information on the teacher's roles and goals, assessment and grouping, choosing texts, instruction, and organization and management. In each area mentioned, the authors provide many helpful reproducibles.

Routman, R. (2002). *Reading essentials: The specifics you need to teach reading well.* Portsmouth, NH: Heinemann.

This book offers practical, research-based strategies for teaching *all* students how to read, including those who struggle. A chapter on guided reading covers topics such as grouping, text selection, management, and scheduling. The appendices include lists of strategies, letters to parents, reading forms, and more.

Chapter 2

The Role of Responsive Guided Reading in the Balanced Literacy Block

"I have 35 students in my first-grade class. I know that guided reading is important, but when am I supposed to do it?"

Differentiating instruction is neither easy nor necessarily intuitive. Many adults were taught largely according to a whole-class, same-lesson, same-text model, so they may have little experience with classrooms that are organized in other ways. The whole-group model works for some students, but it leaves many children behind. For struggling students, whole-group reading instruction can become an exercise in frustration as they fall further and further behind their reading-at-grade-level peers. For advanced students, boredom hits fairly quickly, and their learning goes on either thanks to their own initiative or, often, because they are used to help teach others in the class. These students are not touched by reading instruction that is designed for the middle. It is no longer considered best practice in the teaching of reading to use the same materials and to give the same instruction to each student. We cannot accept teaching only some.

The fact that children have different needs does not mean that there should be no whole-class instruction in reading. Whole-class instruction can and should be part of a *balanced literacy block*. There is much that we can do in whole-group settings. We can introduce new comprehension strategies to students during shared reading, we can build fluency for all of our students by choral reading a great poem, and we can help our students develop a love of literature by ensuring that we read aloud to our classes from great books each and every day. But during whole-group instruction, we cannot provide individualized support to our students. We just can't. And though it may be difficult, this means that no matter how large our class may be, no matter how challenging it may be to get students to work independently so that we can work with small groups, no matter how few reading materials we may have, we must make every effort to work with our students using level-appropriate books on a daily basis, thus addressing the reading needs of each and every student.

THE BALANCED LITERACY BLOCK

Our approach to balanced literacy instruction owes much to the work of Cunningham and Allington (2007) and Routman (2002), among others. Cunningham, Hall, and Sigmon's (2000) four-block model of instruction breaks down the literacy block into the following four areas—self-selected (independent) reading; guided reading (which Cunningham et al. break down into shared reading with the whole-class and small-group guided reading); writing; and word study—and the authors advocate for differentiation within each area. Routman's optimal learning model is intent on moving students from being teacher-dependent to independent readers and writers. Her model begins with teacher demonstration, where teachers explain and model different reading strategies while the whole class listens and observes. Next, teachers involve students more directly through interactive demonstrations where the teacher is still modeling strategies for the whole class but with student feedback and suggestions. The third step is where guided reading occurs, so that students may have time to practice strategies that were taught to the whole class, but in small-group settings with direct support from the teacher. Finally, students have the opportunity to practice the strategy on their own, while they read independently, in books that they can read easily.

Consider a first-grade classroom that is learning about the *ai* pattern for the first time. This model can be conceptualized as in Figure 2.1.

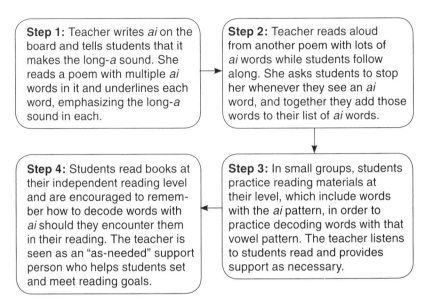

FIGURE 2.1. Relationship among components of balanced literacy.

OUR BALANCED LITERACY MODEL

Borrowing from esteemed educators such as Cunningham and Allington (2007) and Routman (2002), we advocate a literacy block that contains each of the following elements each day:

- Shared reading
- Read-aloud
- Responsive guided reading
- Independent literacy activities
- Word study
- Writing

Shared Reading

Shared reading is the time when teachers work with their whole class to introduce and reinforce new comprehension, vocabulary, or decoding strategies; to share a beloved work of literature; and to encourage discussions about books. For younger students, this is often the time when students gather around the teacher on the rug and follow along as a teacher reads a big book or a nursery rhyme from a poster. This is the time when the teacher is responsible for doing the reading and teaching new concepts. Students will follow along, but ultimately it is the teacher doing the reading. During this time, the teacher typically reads books or materials that would be too difficult for most of the students to read on their own. This is also typically a time when the teacher reads great books in order to engage students with literature.

In kindergarten and first grade, shared reading time can serve multiple purposes. First, by modeling reading a book, turning the pages, and pointing to words as he or she reads, the teacher can model concepts of print and words. This is especially important for students who have not had a lot of exposure to books at home and who may not understand the directionality of print, the distinction between words and illustrations, or the features of books, such as titles, authors, and illustrators. Second, shared reading is a wonderful time for teachers to demonstrate different phonics patterns and show students how those patterns come together in real works of literature. Many kindergarten teachers include short poems in their shared reading instruction, which allows them to focus specifically on certain sounds or patterns in words. Reading poetry during shared reading also allows teachers to focus on areas of phonemic awareness, such as rhyming, that are important for students' phonological development. Finally, shared reading is the ideal time to begin teaching and modeling comprehension strategies. As the reading materials that kindergarten students can read independently tend to be very simplistic, it is important for shared reading to be a time when students are introduced to more complicated texts that require specific strategies for comprehension. It is during shared reading that teachers can explain and model making connections, asking questions, and making predictions. In this way, students learn that reading is not simply about decoding words, but also about making meaning of what we read.

Shared reading is a great time to informally assess students as well. It is during shared reading that teachers can determine who is participating the most and showing the greatest understanding of new concepts. We can quickly see who understands concepts of print by handing students the pointer and asking them to point to each word as the teacher or whole class reads together. We can see who is showing greater phonological awareness by noting who can and cannot answer our questions or point to words with specific sounds. We can also see who is more engaged with literature by observing the faces of our students while we read aloud. Who is listening? Who becomes involved in discussions? Who appears to be (though we can't be sure) checked out because they are rolling around on the rug and seemingly not following along? Shared reading time is a great time to begin to draw some conclusions about our students in order to begin considering how we might place kids in small groups according to their literacy needs.

In second and third grade, shared reading can continue to be a time to introduce new phonics patterns to students, though typically shared reading will focus more on comprehension and vocabulary. Also, in these grades and beyond, shared reading is less likely to involve big book or chart reading, and more likely to be reading that involves multiple copies of the same text that the teacher reads while students follow along. Shared reading in these grades can be a great time to read a novel so that all students can hear and enjoy it while following along, regardless of their reading level. Typically this is an opportune time to demonstrate comprehension strategies and strategies for decoding and understanding unknown, and often multisyllabic, words.

Beyond third grade, shared reading can and should continue, and is an ideal time for teachers to help students learn how to read content-area materials, including textbooks, magazine articles, and other works of nonfiction. Shared reading also remains a great time to do a class reading of a novel or short story so that students who are reading below level can continue to engage and learn from texts beyond their reading level.

Read-Aloud

While shared reading is a time when teachers read with their students in order to provide whole-class strategy instruction, the teacher read-aloud is a time when teachers read largely to share their own love of reading and literature. During a read-aloud, we don't expect our students to respond in any formal way, though a read-aloud can and often does lead to important class discussions. During the read-aloud, our goal is for students to connect with books, to see reading as a relaxing and pleasurable activity, and to build a sense of community. For that reason, we need to be purposeful in the books we select to read aloud. We must consciously choose books that are engaging and that reflect the best of children's literature. While it can be tempting to randomly choose any book from the shelf, it is best to choose books ahead of time, considering students' interests, content-area topics, or issues that have come up in class. It is perfectly fine to read aloud to the students when you unexpectedly have 5 minutes to fill, but it is best to also have a set time for the read-aloud each day. Some teachers read aloud first thing in the morning to bring the classroom community together; immediately after lunch, to settle students back into the school day; or at the very end of the day, setting a relaxing tone during an often hectic time. Kindergarten and first-grade teachers often read aloud multiple times a day—first thing in the morning, after lunch, and at the end of the day—because they know how important it is for their students to be exposed to as much meaningful print as possible.

We believe that the read-aloud is appropriate for all students, from preschool through high school, and we have been disheartened to hear from some of our intermediate teachers that they no longer have time to do a daily read-aloud. In our minds (and supported by research, e.g., Allen, 2000; Anderson, Hiebert, Scott, & Wilkinson, 1985; Beers, 2002; Lesesne, 2003), the read-aloud is essential for building engagement with literature, building classroom community, demonstrating expert reading, and also exposing children to rich vocabulary, multiple text structures, and different cultures and content-area subjects.

Responsive Guided Reading

Based on our observations during shared reading, as well as our more formal assessments of our students, we get a pretty good idea, during the first month of school and throughout the school year, about what our students know and what they still need to learn relative to our literacy instruction. While we can accomplish a lot during whole-class shared reading, we cannot adequately address students' individual literacy needs during that time. Students need to be able to apply what they've learned during whole-class instruction with reading materials that match their abilities with teacher support. Small-group differentiated reading instruction, what we call "responsive guided reading," is an ideal place for that.

Responsive guided reading enables students to receive individualized attention and support from teachers, while using materials that are somewhat challenging for them. During this time, students may practice using a strategy they learned about during shared reading, or they may be encouraged to use additional strategies. The key to responsive guided reading is that teachers can listen to each of their students read, discovering exactly what they are able to do and with what they still struggle. Research (e.g., Block & Pressley, 2002) tells us that this one-on-one time spent with students is the most important and effective activity in influencing literacy development.

Responsive guided reading will look different at different grade levels because children's reading needs and challenges change. We advocate for small-group instruction to begin as early as the fall of kindergarten, though that time will not necessarily involve the reading of books. Rather, as kindergarten teachers get to know their students, they will likely discover that some of their students could benefit from more intensive work on phonemic awareness or phonics. All too often when we observe in kindergarten classrooms, we see whole-class phonemic awareness instruction taking place, where it is clear that as many as half of the students have mastered phonemic awareness and need no more instruction in it. Other students struggle significantly and can't always follow the lesson. Their struggles could be addressed much more efficiently within a small-group setting, where the teacher can focus on their needs and provide individualized help that is more likely to engage students and help them. At the same time, students who no longer need in-depth instruction in phonemic awareness can have their advancing literacy skills addressed as well. So, what we call responsive guided reading instruction may involve reading for some students in kindergarten, but will likely involve word study activities for emergent readers.

Independent Literacy Activities

Independent Reading

Independent reading has two distinct roles in the literacy block. First, it provides children a time to read pleasurable books that they select on their own. While some students come to school with a love of books and will read for pleasure outside of school, some will not. Free reading, DEAR (drop everything and read), SSR (sustained silent reading), and other classifications of the sort should be comfortable and pleasant. It is a time for children to read materials that aren't a struggle and to engage with their own interests. Teachers who believe strongly in free-choice reading often encourage children to learn about selecting texts that they will enjoy: books, periodicals, online reading—any of these can be appropriate for independent reading.

Second, teachers also use independent reading time as a period in the literacy day when students can practice the strategies that have been introduced during shared reading and reinforced during guided reading. Our ultimate goal is that our students will take responsibility for their own reading, and they therefore need to practice reading independently. We encourage teachers to distinguish books that will be read just for the pure joy of reading and those that might be read (still with pleasure) in order to practice something introduced in class. The books used for practice may be slightly more difficult than the ones the students self-select, yet still within their independent, comfortable reading level.

Time spent on independent reading can be approached in different ways. Some teachers have their students read independently while they are working with small groups during responsive guided reading, in lieu of centers. Others make independent reading just one of the literacy activities that take place during guided reading time. Others have a dedicated time where the entire class, including the teacher, read independently. Teachers who have longer blocks of time for literacy sometimes can fit in two different kinds of independent reading, as discussed above. In the first, students read a book or books of their own choosing. In the second, the reading material is teacher-selected.

What is most important to remember about independent reading is that it is the time that students have for independent practice of reading skills and strategies, and it should be a consistent and daily part of the literacy block (Allington & Cunningham, 1996; Blachowicz & Ogle, 2001).

Additional Independent Literacy Activities

In addition to teaching students how to read independently, many teachers also have students work independently on other literacy activities. Using literacy centers or stations, teachers provide independent literacy work for their students to work on while they (the teachers) work with small groups for guided reading. These activities provide time for students to work, at their independent level, on activities that promote phonological awareness, vocabulary growth, and fluency development, as well as writing and literature response. Independent literacy activities, which can be an important part of the literacy block, are addressed in detail in Chapters 6 and 7.

Word Study

Word study is a critical component of learning to read and also to becoming a more accomplished reader. We have included it as its own separate component of the literacy block, but word work can actually be addressed during shared, guided, and independent reading. We think Cunningham and Hall have done amazing work in helping teachers organize word work. We recommend their Making Words series (2008), which includes tips and strategies for teaching phonics, vocabulary and spelling, for grade levels K–5.

Writing

Writing instruction is an often-neglected part of the literacy block, but balanced literacy instruction should include time for writing, both about reading and about the students' own experiences, each day.

Other Literacy Activities

In addition to the fundamental aspects of the literacy block listed above, teachers should also make time, perhaps less regularly, for literacy activities such as literature circles, instruction in research, and Readers' Theatre.

PUTTING IT ALL TOGETHER

There is a lot to consider when planning literacy instruction each day. Examples A and B provide a look at a model literacy block plan for kindergarten and third grade, assuming that teachers offer 90 minutes of literacy instruction each day.

Example A: Kindergarten Literacy Block

9:00–9:30	Circle time/shared reading; morning read-aloud; morning message; shared reading using the big book *Is Your Mama a Llama?*, focusing on rhyming words.
9:30–10:00	Responsive guided reading—two groups for 15 minutes each.
9:30–10:00	Independent literacy activities
10:00–10:30	Writing time, beginning with whole-group interactive writing, followed by independent practice with teacher support.

Mrs. Johansson calls the students over to the rug to begin the day. Typically, she begins her literacy block on the rug because so much of the beginning-of-the-day activities involve literacy. Students take the popsicle stick with their name and picture on it and move it to a can marked "hot lunch" or "sack lunch." In this way, the teacher can easily see who is present that day and who will be getting a hot lunch. This is done in a matter of minutes so that the morning read-aloud can begin. Today, Mrs. Johansson is reading *My Little Sister Ate One Hare* by Bill Grossman (1998). She chooses this book because she has been working on rhyming with her students, and this book has humorous rhymes. Even more importantly, though, Mrs. Johansson chooses it because, with a story line about the unusual things the main character eats, the book never fails to captivate her students and make them laugh. Her goal for her morning read-aloud is to start the day with her students fully engaged in reading. After the read-aloud, Mrs. Johansson shares that day's morning message, which says, "Good morning, Room 14! Today is Monday, October 24th. We have art today. We have P.E. today. Today we will think of words that rhyme with *cat*." Mrs. Johansson calls up Letitia to point to the words in the morning message while she reads them aloud. She then reads the message again, encouraging the students to read along with her the second time around. She asks students to think of words that rhyme with *cat* and offers a marker so that students can attempt to write those words down. Mrs. Johansson learns a lot from this activity, as she can see who is able to follow along with the words of the message, who is able to think of rhyming words, and who is able to begin to write those words.

Next, Mrs. Johansson shows the students the big book *Is Your Mama a Llama?* by Deborah Guarino. She takes them on a picture walk of the book, and then explains that the lines of the book will rhyme. She demonstrates this by reading the first several pages of the book and repeating the rhyming words. She reads the next few pages and asks the students if they can identify the rhyming words. Finally, she reads the sentence that contains the first rhyming word, then pauses before reading the final rhyming word to see if students can identify the word before she reads it. She encourages them to look at the letters in the word to help them. The book is fun and engaging, and most students are actively involved in discerning the rhymes.

After shared reading, Mrs. Johansson explains that she will be meeting with Group A and Group B today, while the rest of the students work in centers. There are four centers in the room. The first is the library center, where students bring their book boxes with preselected independent reading books and settle in comfortably for reading. The second center is the word work center which today has word sorts of varying levels of difficulty, including an initial sound word sort, a final consonant sound word sort, and a short-*a* word family sort. The third center is the writing center, where students are encouraged to either draw a picture and label it, to the best of their ability, or to cut a picture out of a pile of magazines to label. The fourth center is the listening center, where students put on headphones and listen to a book on tape.

While students are working in centers, Mrs. Johansson calls up Group A. The students in this group are those students who still seem to be struggling to hear rhymes in words. Even during today's shared reading, she observed that these students either did not respond when asked for an appropriate rhyming word or provided words that did not rhyme. Clearly they aren't ready to engage in whole text reading on the model of responsive guided reading. Instead, Mrs. Johansson works with them in their group on skills she knows they will need to lead them toward whole word, page, and text reading. It is likely that later in the year their group will more closely resemble a responsive guided reading group that one would see in a first-grade classroom. After 15 minutes, Mrs. Johansson sends Group A to the independent reading center and calls Group B over to the guided reading table. Each other group rotates to the next center. Group B has demonstrated a solid understanding of phonemic awareness, so Mrs. Johansson is currently working with them on different phonics patterns. Today they are reading a book called *The Fat Cat Sat on the Mat* by Nurit Karlin, which includes different short-*a* word families. She helps the students decode and use strategies for sight word recognition as they work through this text on the responsive guided reading model.

After 15 minutes, guided reading/independent literacy activity time is over. Mrs. Johansson calls the class back to the rug to begin an interactive writing activity. In keeping with the work they've already done, they are working on writing a class poem. Mrs. Johansson gets them started by giving them a beginning line: "I'm so happy I could _____." She calls on Liam to fill in the blank. He thinks for a moment and says, "Scream." She hands him the marker and asks him to think about what sound he hears at the beginning. "/S/," he replies and she asks him to write that down. She asks him to think about the sound he hears at the end of the word, and he shrugs. She emphasizes, "ScreaMMM." He replies, "/R/?" She makes a mental note that Liam needs to work on ending sounds with Group A. Many students are called up to help write the rhyming words in the poem they create together.

The literacy block ends with students writing in their writers notebooks. Mrs. Johansson encourages students to attempt to write words or sentences that rhyme, but explains that they can also draw a picture and label it.

Example B: Third-Grade Literacy Block

9:00–9:15	Shared reading: *Sarah, Plain and Tall*. Teacher reads aloud while students follow along. Teacher explains the comprehension strategy of visualizing and demonstrates how he creates a visual picture as he reads the description of the farmland on which the story takes place.
9:15–9:45	Responsive guided reading—two groups for 15 minutes each; students reminded of visualization strategy before they read.
9:15–9:45	Independent reading and independent literacy activities.
9:45–10:30	Writing workshop: mini-lesson on revising the lead, then half hour for independent writing and conferencing with teacher.

Mr. Peters asks the students to take out their copies of *Sarah, Plain and Tall* by Patricia MacLachlan, which is part of their social studies unit on pioneers. He tells them that one thing good readers do when they read is to create a picture in their head of the descriptions the author provides of the setting or a character. He explains that in *Sarah, Plain and Tall*, the setting plays a very important part in the story, and to help him visualize it more effectively, he sometimes closes his eyes and tries to really see it. He tells them to turn to page 5 and read along as he reads the following passage: "Outside the prairie reached out and touched the places where the sky came down. Though winter was nearly over, there were patches of snow and ice everywhere. I looked at the long dirt road that crawled across the plains, remembering the morning that Mama had died, cruel and sunny." Mr. Peters demonstrates how he closes his eyes in order to see the setting better. He thinks aloud,

> "I wonder what it means when the author says the prairie reached out and touched the places where the sky comes down. When I think about what that means, I remember that the prairie is very flat and you can see for miles around you. I think Anna is looking way out over the prairie to the place where the land and the sky seem to meet."

He tells them that while he reads today, he would like them to create their own pictures of the author's descriptions. He talks at several places during the reading and asks different students to describe the pictures in their heads.

After 15 minutes of shared reading, Mr. Peters asks the students to put away their books and look at the guided reading/independent literacy activity schedule for the day to determine what they're going to do during this time. While he's working with the responsive guided reading groups, the students will be engaging in different independent literacy activities: independent reading, letter writing, making big words, and buddy reading. Mr. Peters's first group is about a year below grade level, and today he has chosen a DRA level-24 book from the book room in the school, *Zoom* by Robert Munsch. He reminds them to create a picture in their heads while they read descriptive passages to better understand what's going on in the book. However, he knows that they will likely miscue or struggle in different places and on different words, so he keeps his prereading instruction to a bare minimum. He listens to each individual student read, and provides support when he or she miscues or when meaning appears to break down. After 15 minutes, he calls the next group and reminds the rest of the class that it is time to move on to the next independent literacy activity. The next guided reading group, though reading more challenging materials, moves at about the same pace as the previous group.

Mr. Peters reminds students to clean up after themselves and to come sit down at their desks. He teaches a 10-minute lesson on creating exciting leads, using his own writing as an example of both good and bad leads. After the mini-lesson, he asks students to take out their own writing workshop pieces and to read through and consider revising the lead they have already written. He tells them that they have about half an hour to write before they need to go to P.E. He circulates through the room, monitoring writing progress and providing on-the-spot conferences when needed. After writing, the students have to go to music class, but Mr. Peters makes time before lunch to read aloud each day. Currently, to go with the pioneer theme, he has been reading aloud from the informational book *Growing up in Pioneer America: 1800–1890* by Judith Pinkerton Josephson.

We encourage teachers to keep a balanced literacy approach in mind as they plan their literacy instruction each week. We emphasize that as students get older, certain parts of the block may change, and even day to day and week to week certain areas may receive greater emphasis than others. However, keeping in mind Routman's (2002) model for gradual release of responsibility, we believe that including time for shared, guided, and independent reading, as well as writing instruction, will provide instruction that best meets the needs of all

EACH DAY

Activity	How long	Books/ materials	What prep?
Independent reading (IR)			
Guided reading (GR)			
Independent literacy activities (ILA)			
Reading aloud (RA)			
Writing			
Writing workshop (WW)			
Other writing (OW)			
Shared reading instruction (SR) (comprehension/vocabulary)			
Word work (phonemic awareness, phonics, spelling strategies)			
Other language arts (Readers' Theatre, research, study skills, and literature circles)			

EACH WEEK

Monday	Tuesday	Wednesday	Thursday	Friday
IR	IR	IR	IR	IR
GR	GR	GR	GR	GR
ILA	ILA	ILA	ILA	ILA
RA	RA	RA	RA	RA
WW	OW	WW	OW	WW
SR Comp	SR Vocab	SR Comp	SR Vocab	SR Comp
Word work	Word work	Word work	Word work	Word work
Other LA (?)	Other LA (?)	Other LA (?)	Other LA (?)	Other LA (?)

EACH MONTH

Week 1	Week 2	Week 3	Week 4
Above (+)	Above (+)	Above (+)	Above (+)
Readers' Theatre	Research	Study skills	Literature circles

FIGURE 2.2. Planning the literacy block.

students at all grade levels. Figure 2.2 is a planning guide we use with teachers to help them plan for balanced literacy instruction each day, each week, and over the course of a month. We find that this helps teachers see when they've been neglecting an area of the balanced literacy block, and it also helps them to see how they can plan their time most efficiently. For example, knowing that shared reading is an important part of the literacy block, yet faced with insufficient time for literacy instruction, some teachers elect to do shared reading during social studies or science instruction.

RESOURCES FOR FURTHER READING

Allington, R. L., & Cunningham, P. M. (1996). *Schools that work: Where all children read and write.* New York: HarperCollins.

These authors are passionate in their view that our schools need to change in order to better serve *all* children. They explain why large blocks of time should be allotted for reading and writing, and how to best serve students with special needs within such a framework. One chapter takes the reader on a tour through a school that works in which we see guided reading, writing mini-lessons, and self-selection of texts.

Cunningham, P. M., & Allington, R. L. (2007). *Classrooms that work: They can all read and write* (4th ed.). Boston: Allyn & Bacon.

This book presents guided reading as an integral component of a balanced literacy program. This updated edition provides teachers with workable, practical strategies and activities for their K–8 reading programs. Included are chapters that describe a sample day in a building blocks kindergarten, a sample day in a four-blocks primary classroom, and a sample week in a big blocks intermediate classroom.

Cunningham, P. M., Hall, D. P., & Sigmon, C. M. (2000). *The teacher's guide to the four blocks: A multimethod, multilevel framework for grades 1–3.* Greensboro, NC: Carson-Dellosa.

This book explains how guided reading fits into the four-blocks framework. The chapters devoted to guided reading clearly explain what guided reading is and offer ideas about how to implement it effectively in classrooms, grades K–3. There is an excellent frequently asked questions section at the end of the book, which attempts to answer questions such as "How do you get it all done?" and "How do you give grades?"

Hall, D. P., & Williams, E. (2000). *The teacher's guide to building blocks: A developmentally appropriate multilevel framework for kindergarten.* Greensboro, NC: Carson-Dellosa.

This book explains how to bring the four-blocks model into a kindergarten classroom. Chapters such as "Reading to Children," "Reading with Children," and "Reading by Children" provide activities sure to prepare children for guided reading experiences. A list of dozens of recommended read-aloud books for kindergartners is also included.

Pearson, D. P., Raphael, T. E., Benson, V. L., & Madda, C. L. (2007). Balance in comprehensive literacy instruction: Then and now. In L. B. Gambrell, L. M. Morrow, & M. Pressley (Eds.), *Best practices in literacy instruction* (3rd ed., pp. 30–56). New York: Guilford Press.

This chapter discusses the need for balanced comprehensive literacy instruction in the United States. The authors define *balanced* and explain why it refers to far more than whether educators take a whole-language or phonics-based approach. They explain that educators must "shift the debates about balance *away* from single-dimension discussions of what to teach and what not to teach, and *toward* the notion that achieving a balanced literacy curriculum is a logical goal of all literacy educators."

Pressley, M. (2006). *Reading instruction that works: The case for balanced teaching* (3rd ed.). New York: Guilford Press.

The author presents updated information on best practices for the balanced literacy block. Especially enlightening is the chapter titled "Expert Primary-Level Teaching of Literacy," which discusses the research on distinguishing characteristics of the best primary reading teachers. This third edition includes new research as well as three new chapters on fluency, vocabulary, and writing.

Routman, R. (2002). *Reading essentials: The specifics you need to teach reading well.* Portsmouth, NH: Heinemann.

This book offers practical, research-based strategies for teaching *all* students how to read, including those who struggle. There is a chapter on guided reading, which covers topics such as grouping, text selection, management, and scheduling. The appendices include lists of strategies, letters to parents, reading forms, and more.

Chapter 3

A Detailed Look
at Responsive Guided Reading

*"Everyone in my school says they do guided
reading but every time I observe a group,
it looks different. Is there some kind
of standard way of doing things?"*

We hope that after reading Chapters 1 and 2 new teachers and teachers new to guided reading might understand why guided reading is an important component of balanced literacy and where it fits in an elementary literacy block. Understanding the justification for guided reading is a necessary component of good literacy instruction, but not enough to be an effective teacher of guided reading. In this chapter, we detail the ways in which teachers can function in a *responsive* guided reading group so that students are maximally instructed and teacher time is minimally taxed. In this chapter we take for granted the *why* and the *where* and concentrate on the *how*.

You may recall from Chapter 1 that some of the characteristics of a responsive guided reading group are the following: (1) it follows a predictable, transparent structure; (2) the teacher waits for the student to miscue before determining what to teach; (3) groups must be brief enough so that the rest of the class can manage unsupervised (more on this topic in Chapters 6 and 7); and (4) the teacher can meet with enough groups per week so that all children are getting this quality instruction on a regular basis. These characteristics are the ones we wish to discuss in this chapter.

SHORT, RESPONSIVE, AND PREDICTABLE:
THE RESPONSIVE GUIDED READING GROUP

As we noted in Chapter 1, children and teachers benefit from routine. Teachers who feel overwhelmed by the idea of teaching in small groups are often relieved to know that responsive guided reading groups are run in the same, specific way each time. The wild card is always, of course, the errors that children make (discussed below), but there is a great comfort in knowing how the structure will operate. We believe that following a consistent structure liberates teachers and learners to be more creative in their teaching and learning. We offer a structure that has been successful for us when working with teachers unused to this kind of differentiated teaching, but we offer it only as a model, with the hopes that teachers will develop their own individualized structure with which they can feel comfortable. Our structure is one that is designed to move quickly into the most important part of the group: listening to children read. We often observe teachers in guided reading groups spending a great deal of time on prefatory remarks, preteaching, querying students, and setting up background for the book. Our model is reliant upon the student reading as the basis for the instructional decision making, so this kind of opening is kept to the barest minimum. The steps are listed and discussed below. Approximate timings are in parentheses following each step.

1. Brief introduction (less than 30 seconds).
2. Teacher reads (30 seconds).
3. Children chorally read with teacher (30 seconds).
4. Children are directed to continue to read silently or to whisper read (30 seconds).
5. Teacher circulates to each child, listening to him or her read and providing customized cueing (2 minutes per child x 5 children = 10 minutes).
6. Teacher asks children to stop reading (30 seconds).
7. Teacher summarizes the strategy he or she worked on with each child and asks him or her to say it back (5 minutes).
8. Teacher calls the next groups and repeats Steps 1–7.

As you can see, this entire group experience takes between 15 and 20 minutes. If the teacher sticks very closely to this schedule, he or she will be able to successfully meet with two groups per day without an enormous tax on the independent working ability of the rest of the class. Each of the steps is discussed in greater detail below.

Step 1: Introduction

It has been our observation that teachers often spend a large amount of time preparing students to read once they have been called into their guided reading groups. We have seen teachers spend time helping children to activate prior knowledge; helping them to predict what might happen in the text based on the cover photograph, art, and/or title; pre-teaching vocabulary; helping them to anticipate difficulties with phonics rules; teaching word recognition strategies; and more. We want to be clear that we believe these are valuable activities in an overall plan for teaching reading to children. We instruct our preservice teachers in how to work with children on all of these skills and strategies. We just don't spend a good deal of time preparing students to work on them in this teaching context, in the responsive guided reading group.

We see the time in a responsive guided reading group as limited and precious, and as such we try to spend time doing those things that cannot be done in the whole group. For example, if teachers would like children to learn how to use clues from the title page of a book to help ready them for reading, they can discuss and model this strategy just as easily in front of the whole class as they can in a small group. If they wish to teach children to relate their background knowledge to the topic of the text, similarly, they can spend a series of whole-group mini-lessons doing just that. If they believe children are ready to look for "little words inside the big words" or understand that "when two vowels go walking the first one does the talking," there is time in the literacy day to teach these strategies. Again, we encourage instruction in these reading skills because they have been shown to build fluency, provide a purpose and a context for reading, and help children to attend to and construct meaning more fruitfully. Additionally, we hope that children bring these skills and strategies to the reading they do in a responsive guided reading group. If, however, we spend time on this kind of instruction with a small group, we miss out on the benefits of working with just a single student at a time.

We think that the focus of responsive guided reading should be contextual cueing for individual students, that is, individual support to children for one or a very small number of errors. The teacher learns what cues children need by listening to them read individually. If teachers do not move to this activity very quickly, their groups may run too long, risking the disintegration of the behavior of the rest of the class, and ultimately making it difficult to maintain responsive guided reading as a regular part of classroom literacy instruction. We always ask teachers to consider, "If you can do it in whole-group instruction, does it need to be a focus in the small group?"

It is true that teachers will find that small groups sometimes need one kind of instruction while others need other kinds. For instance, in a first-grade classroom it would be very typical to have a group of five or so children who are learning to decode multisyllabic words while another group is still struggling with long and short vowel sounds. You might find a fourth-grade teacher who wishes to work on inferential predictions with one group and literal predictions with another. Many teachers use the time in a guided reading group to provide this kind of needed instruction, and we see why this would make sense. We hope, though, that teachers could arrange other opportunities to do this kind of instruction, perhaps pulling groups or working with individual students during independent reading time. It would be ideal to have time for this kind of small-group differentiated reading instruction as well as having time for responsive guided reading groups. We know that with limited time, this may be unrealistic, but we believe that offering the ideal gives us something to work toward.

Instead, then, of lengthy introductions and discussions, we ask teachers to remind students of a strategy to which they have previously been introduced in a whole group, one that may very well support their reading of the book. We ask teachers not to spend time planning this introduction, but instead to make it a natural continuation of a conversation that has been going on in the classroom. Some examples of what actual teachers have said to start the groups can be found in Figure 3.1.

As you can see from these examples, this introduction is kept to a minimum because the teacher is not introducing new strategies, but rather just reminding students of discussions they have had previously. This is effective as it allows students to think about applying a concept taught earlier in the day, the week, the month, or the year.

STEP 2: Teacher Reads

Because we like to have the groups structured the same each time, we have the teacher read for about 30 seconds aloud to the group, while the students follow along in their copies. For a kindergarten or first-grade teacher, this might be a large chunk of the book because there may be very few words on a page. If this is the case, we ask the teacher

From a second-grade teacher:

"I picked this book for you and I think it might be a real challenge because there are so many words on a page. Do you remember that we have been talking about looking only at small chunks of text at a time? That will help."

From a first-grade teacher:

"Remember that there are several things you can do when you come to a word you don't know. You can look at the first letter and then the picture to see if it helps. You can take a running start, or you can think of a word that might just fit the rest of the sentence that looks a little like the unknown word. Those are three strategies you might try as you read today."

From a fifth-grade teacher:

"This book has charts, it has graphs, it has photos, it has captions, it has maps, and it has boxes. We might not read it from top to bottom. We could decide to start with some of the graphics as that might help make the text easier to understand."

FIGURE 3.1. Sample teacher language to begin groups.

to just read a page or two. This helps the students get ready for the rest of the group work and gives them an initial model of fluent reading.

STEP 3: Children Read Chorally with Teacher

For a very short time, we like to have the students read together with the teacher. This serves as a warm-up as they prepare to read independently. Usually, the teacher will adjust his or her volume so he or she is reading just above the volume of the group. This way, each student hears the teacher and his or her own reading. We know that children benefit very little from listening to the reading of their peers when the reading they are doing is slow-going for them, as it is designed to be in a responsive guided reading group.

STEP 4: Children Are Directed to Continue to Read Silently or to Whisper Read and Are Instructed on What to Do If They Finish Reading before the Teacher Is Available to Them

We build directions about procedures into the structure of the group. It is helpful to students to be reminded of how to behave and what they can do when they finish. Teachers might say, "Okay, remember that I will listen to you all read, but as you wait for me, or after I have already read with you, you will want to read to yourself very quietly in a whisper or silently in your head." It is very important, for the smooth execution of the group, that children know what to do if they find themselves racing through the text and are finished before the teacher gets to them or what to do if they are among the first to read and finish before the teacher has completed listening to all group members. Teachers have great success with relatively simple "after-reading" activities. For example, primary teachers might place paper and markers in the middle of the table and tell students to color a picture of their favorite part of the book if they finish early. Intermediate teachers might provide sticky notes and provide a directive such as "Mark a place in the book that you particularly liked and write why on the sticky note."

It is true that the text may prove more difficult than some students can really struggle through on their own, and they become frustrated. If this is the case, it may be just as well for them to do some writing or other quiet activity while they await the arrival of the teacher and his or her support. (Note that this may also indicate that the material is beyond the instructional level of the student and may necessitate a group change for that student. More information on this topic is provided in Chapter 9.)

New teachers often ask us what to do about the child who elects to listen to the group member who is reading to the teacher and the subsequent conversation that the teacher might have with that child. We think there are far worse things than having one student listen to another student learn as long as he or she is not intrusive to either that student or the teacher. This kind of "remote" teaching can be helpful and efficient.

STEP 5: Teacher Circulates to Each Child, Listening to Them Read and Providing Customized Cueing

This step is the essence of the responsive guided reading group. The most important reason to draw children together in this way is to have the opportunity for the teacher to hear them read on their own. There is no better information about how a child is reading than listening to him or her read by him- or herself and having the luxury of attending only to him or her. It is amazing how much one can learn about a child's reading ability in just a minute listening to him or her read. The books chosen for responsive guided reading groups are chosen because they will force students to miscue in fairly short order. For beginning readers, they will likely miscue on a word they are almost ready to read fluently or strategically; for a more advanced reader, they will likely reveal a breakdown in comprehension or vocabulary knowledge. We want students to reveal a breakdown in decoding or understanding so that the teacher can provide a prompt that they might use to help them in this text, and much more importantly, a strategy they might employ in the future when they come to something they do not understand or recognize.

We will discuss the kinds of cues that teachers often provide for beginning and more advanced readers in the next two chapters (Chapters 4 and 5). In this chapter, we would like to solidify the timing and practices of the teachers and the students. We ask teachers to circulate to the students because it minimizes disruption of their reading and offers a slight measure of privacy not available if the teacher listens from his or her traditional seat at the opposite end of the table from all the children. Remember that all the children are reading as the teacher listens to just one at a time, in serial fashion. While it isn't possible to keep the out-loud reader from distracting all the others, we try to keep it to a minimum by bringing the teacher as close to the child who is reading as possible. Many teachers kneel; others drag a chair around the perimeter of the table, slightly behind the child who is reading.

Timing on this step is important as it easily can turn into 5 or more minutes per child, which then increases the time in this one group to far too long to maintain peace in the rest of the class. In addition, it reduces the likelihood that the teacher will be able to meet with two groups in the allotted time. If the child reads along for more than a minute or so without miscuing, the teacher may conclude that the book he or she selected is not difficult enough for the child to use in this context. He or she might say, "You are reading beautifully. I am sorry I picked a book that you could read just fine without me. Next time, I will come up with something harder so you and I can really work." This is preferable to having the child continue reading or by trying to come up with something to teach that the child's reading did not demand. Generally, though, the child will miscue quickly. Once the teacher has listened to the child's reading and provided at least one cue, the teacher moves onto the next child in the group. This portion of the responsive guided reading group is finished when each child in the group has had an opportunity to be heard.

This is often the most intimidating part of the responsive guided reading group. Teachers must learn to listen very carefully to students as they read in order to provide them with appropriate support. Our experience shows that teachers improve at this skill the more they do it and that there are various supports that can help them. For example, it is true that student miscues will vary, but there are a small number of cues that help with many errors. Common cues for early and fluent readers can be found in Chapters 4 and 5. New teachers often write these most common cues on a 3" × 5" card and keep the card handy as they listen to students read. Once teachers have worked with responsive guided reading groups for a while, they may want to alter the list to reflect the needs of their individual students. Similarly, it can be extremely helpful for new teachers to observe experienced teachers or literacy coaches running guided reading groups so that they can hear the kinds of cues provided to students. It is important that teachers be generous to themselves and their own learning curve. Nobody is an expert at cueing at the start. We will provide help in the next chapters, but perhaps the greatest help is to know that there is no perfect cue, and that even the most imperfect cue helps the teacher to learn about student reading.

STEP 6: Teacher Asks Children to Stop Reading

Once the teacher has listened to each student read, he or she returns to his or her spot and asks students to close their books. Responsive guided reading groups sometimes read the same book for two or more meetings, and sometimes do not. The point of this step is to bring the group back together for the ending portion of the group.

STEP 7: Teacher Summarizes the Strategy He or She Worked on with Each Child and Asks Them to Say It Back

As we have talked to teachers and students over the years, we have noticed that students are sometimes quite adept at using skills or strategies under the watchful eye of the teacher, yet struggle to do so when they are at their desks, reading at home, or looking at texts outside of "reading" (e.g., content-area textbooks, periodicals). One important element of the responsive guided reading group is helping children to transfer the cue given by the teacher to their future reading. It is probably true that giving a child a single strategy once will be ineffective in transferring, yet a teacher who repeats a cue to a student several times might very well help the student to integrate the practice. Because it is quite possible that students will miscue in the same manner over time, the cues get repeated. We talk to teachers about giving students the metaphor of "putting the strategy in your pocket," that is, taking the strategy with them when they leave the table. We think it is important that the strategy be practiced as soon as possible so that students begin to build it into their repertoire of things they do when word recognition or understanding break down. In order to facilitate this, the final segment of the responsive guided reading group is a discussion and reinforcement of what happened as each child read. The teacher might go child by child and ask, "What did we work on when we read together?," or, if more than one child worked on a similar strategy or skill, the teacher might chunk them together. An example of a closing segment from a second-grade class can be found in the next section. Following each child's restatement of the instruction, the teacher asks the child to "put that into your pocket" (sometimes literally writing it out for him or her on a yellow sticky note and handing it to him or her) and "try to use it next time you come to a word, sentence, or passage that is difficult."

TRANSCRIPT OF AN ENDING SEGMENT IN A SECOND-GRADE CLASSROOM

MRS. ROSEN: Marta, why don't you tell me what we worked on when we read together?

MARTA: You said that if I come to a big word like the one we came to that I should put my finger over part of it to see if that helps me to get it.

MRS. ROSEN: That is right, so for the rest of today and tomorrow, I want you to seek out big words and try that as much as you can. Don't be frustrated if it doesn't always work. Keep trying. Okay, Jordan and Lauren, I think we worked on the same thing. Lauren, why don't you remind us."

LAUREN: You said to sometimes pronounce the -ed at the end of words like /d/ instead of /ed/.

MRS. ROSEN: Right. Jordan, you and Lauren worked on the same word. Do you remember what it was?

JORDAN: *Slapp-ed*, I mean *slapped*.

MRS. ROSEN: Good. Now I want both of you, Lauren and Jordan, to look out for words that end in an *-ed*. You should know that if it doesn't sound like a word that is familiar to you, then perhaps you are saying it wrong and you might try just /d/ for instance. Most words will be familiar to you, so if they are not, really think about them. Okay? Next time we meet, can you bring me some *-ed* ending words? Now, Claire, do you remember our discussion?

CLAIRE: We talked about how when I read I can pause and take a breath when I see a comma and that might help me understand better.

MRS. ROSEN: Exactly right. So you will be a comma pauser all day today and tomorrow as you read?

CLAIRE: Okay.

MRS. ROSEN: And finally, Anthony. You read quite a while before you struggled. But right there at the end we worked on what ... ?

ANTHONY: You said that sometimes words look like other words that I might know. So I hadn't seen the word *flight* but I know the word *fight* so I just added an *l*.

MRS. ROSEN: So, a really good thing to do is look at words you don't know and see if the patterns of the letters are of words that you do know. I hope you will do that all day today and tomorrow too. If you find one, let me know.

In the example above, Mrs. Rosen has a brief conversation with each child, reinforcing the lesson and letting others hear what teaching might have gone on. This allows these students, at times, to benefit from instruction custom-designed for another student. Teachers hope that repetition of this kind of instruction over time will secure the idea for students that words, sentences, and texts should make sense, and that if they do not, there are strategies one can try and good readers have many from which to draw.

Clearly, running an effective responsive guided reading group takes skill and practice. We believe the time invested in teaching children and teachers to work in this special instructional context is well worth it. The next section provides a much more in-depth look at teacher cueing, both of beginning readers (in Chapter 4) and of fluent readers (in Chapter 5).

RESOURCES FOR FURTHER READING

Dorn, L., French, C., & Jones, T. (1998). *Apprenticeship in literacy: Transitions across reading and writing*. Portland, ME: Stenhouse.

The authors explain how to implement an apprenticeship approach to literacy in K–3 classrooms. Educators will learn how to support students in a balanced literacy program, and how to withdraw that support as students gain independence. A chapter on guided reading discusses emergent, early, and fluent guided reading.

Fountas, I. C., & Pinnell, G. S. (2008). *When readers struggle: Teaching that works*. Portsmouth, NH: Heinemann.

This book is filled with specific teaching ideas for helping children who are having difficulty reading and writing in grades K–3. The authors discuss small-group interventions and individual interactions during reading and writing. There are specific chapters devoted to problem solving, independence, fluency, and comprehending in reading. There is also a chapter that presents 15 keys to effective intervention.

Pinnell, G. S., & Fountas, I. C. (2007). *The continuum of literacy learning, grades K–2: A guide to teaching*. Portsmouth, NH: Heinemann.

The first half of this book provides educators with a continuum of literacy goals for each grade level, K–2, across seven curricular areas. The second half provides goals appropriate for each text level, A–N. It also guides educators in how to select texts effectively at each level. These continua will help educators plan small-group instruction, identify specific needs for targeted intervention, and assess literacy development in students grades K–2.

Pinnell, G. S., & Fountas, I. C. (2007). *The continuum of literacy learning, grades 3–8: A guide to teaching*. Portsmouth, NH: Heinemann.

The first half of this book provides educators with a continuum of literacy goals for each grade level, 3–8, across seven curricular areas. The second half provides goals appropriate for each text level, L–Z. It also guides educators in how to select texts effectively at each level. These continua will help educators plan small-group instruction, identify specific needs for targeted intervention, and assess literacy development in students grades 3–8.

Part II

Teacher Cueing in Responsive Guided Reading Groups

Chapter 4

Prompting Beginning Readers during Responsive Guided Reading

"When my students miscue,
I never know exactly what to say.... "

As we have discussed in previous chapters, the most important component of the responsive guided reading group is that the teacher listen to the students as they read. It is rare for teachers to have the opportunity to listen to students read aloud, by themselves. Even when teachers have every intention of wandering around during whole-group reading and listening to students read, it is likely that they will not get to enough students so that all are heard in the course of a week. The responsive guided reading group is a context that ensures that every student will have the chance to have this individualized attention on a regular basis.

There is little preplanning in a responsive guided reading group because the students in many ways "tell" the teacher what strategies they are in need of by the miscues they make and the puzzling through (or not puzzling through) that the teacher observes when the miscues occur. This has both helpful and difficult elements. On the helpful side, this kind of instruction means the teacher devotes much less time to planning guided reading lessons; on the difficult side, this kind of instruction means the teacher has to do much more on-the-spot teaching, which can be unnerving at first.

To illustrate, imagine that a teacher has selected a text for a responsive guided reading group that is at the group's instructional level. This teacher goes through the first brief steps detailed in Chapter 3, and then proceeds to listen to each child read. The teacher doesn't know what miscues each child will make, and it is more than likely that in a group of five students (even when they are at the same level), the miscues will be different. Thus the teacher has to be prepared to respond to student miscues, or breakdowns in understanding, without exact knowledge of or preparation for what those might be.

Many of the teachers we work with believe that once they get their groups going, good instruction will fall into place. We wish that were the case, but we know for certain that effective prompting, that is, responding to student errors by offering strategic hints, takes knowledge and practice. Schwarz (2005) has found that it is this aspect of guided reading that is most challenging for teachers. His research indicates that teachers have no trouble with the before and after reading portions of guided reading, but rather struggle during student reading, when they have to make decisions quickly in order to best scaffold students.

> The task becomes more complex as teachers try to provide immediate feedback as they listen to one student or a group of students reading the story aloud. This is the type of guidance that many struggling readers need to construct problem-solving strategies on the run as they read. Guided reading lessons give us the opportunity to provide this type of support. (Schwarz, 2005, p. 436)

Clay (2001) acknowledges that teachers are likely underprepared to understand the kinds of support that will best help our struggling students to make progress. Cole (2006) says, "Teachers must have a broad spectrum of internalized cues for use with scaffolding—ones they can employ at a moment's notice. Devoid of such internalized options, teachers overuse and abuse particular cues, such as 'sound it out' or 'tell' " (p. 451).

With that said, we also know that no student failed to learn to read because a teacher gave him or her the wrong prompt or because a teacher, on a given day, didn't know what to say. Teachers must give themselves the freedom to be learners also, to try out prompting students, to think carefully about the practice, and then strive to improve. It is true that teachers get better at this quite quickly but that all novices feel uncomfortable and worried that students might make a miscue to which they will not know how to respond. As reasonable as this worry is, it isn't a reason not to try.

The new teachers we have worked with have found it helpful to review the kinds of prompts they are most likely to give before they sit down with groups. Even though any grade level will have a wide spectrum of abilities, there are very common miscues that students make, and thus teachers can prepare themselves to respond to these miscues. In this chapter we discuss prompting for word recognition, the kind of prompting usually done in the lower grades (K–3) but that will extend into the upper grades for struggling students. We also offer a list of prompts and advice about how a teacher might think about using them. In the next chapter we talk about prompting fluent readers.

We wish to make it clear that we believe comprehension and vocabulary learning should begin in earnest in the primary grades. We want kids listening to stories, thinking about words, and reading and writing to reinforce these vital skills. In our balanced literacy block (as discussed in Chapter 2) there is plenty of time to work with students on these components of reading. We also believe that much of this work can be done more effectively in teaching contexts other than guided reading groups. In the lower grades, or until children are fluent readers, we use responsive guided reading groups to prompt word recognition, to help students get this important skill down as solidly and quickly as they can so that they can devote their full cognitive energy to meaning making without having to stop and decode, explicitly invoke sight words, or use semantic clues to discern unknown words.

Teachers are sometimes frustrated because they provide what they believe to be a reasonable cue and the child still cannot get the unknown word at hand. The purpose of a guided reading group is to force a child to miscue so that the teacher can model and/or advise the child on what to do if this happens again. This process, therefore, is not successful or unsuccessful based on that one miscue and how the teacher or student responds. Rather, that miscue is generally representative of a lack of strategy that the teacher can then begin to work on with the child. One cue won't usually solve much, but the repetition of a strategy over time will help a child move to independent use of that strategy, the ultimate goal of reading instruction. The scaffold provided by the teacher is there not necessarily for the purpose of figuring out this one word, but as an example of how a student might analyze any unknown word.

The goal of cueing in guided reading is transferability over texts and time. A teacher shouldn't feel that instruction has not been effective just because the child was unable to apply it to the word at hand in that moment. We would much rather have the child learn a strategy that can be used outside the guided reading group then have the child be successful with the one word he or she works on with the teacher and then never be able to invoke the strategy again. It is also worth remembering that children must practice strategies multiple times before they begin to incorporate them into their repertoire of things to do when they come to an unknown word. Teachers are wise to set up multiple opportunities for children to make the same kinds of errors (in small groups, large group, pairs, and independently) over time so that they get used to using a strategy or set of strategies.

PROMPTING WORD RECOGNITION

It is widely known that teachers are most comfortable with teaching practices that they experienced themselves as students. Lortie (1975) calls this an "apprenticeship of observation" and cites this as a major barrier to teachers embracing contemporary notions of teaching and learning. It is just very hard, Lortie argues, to break the notion that what was done to us may not be the most appropriate in all cases. In short, generally, what was done to "us" is what we do to "them" despite our best intentions. It is most likely that our recollection of being prompted to figure out unknown words was with the phrase "Sound it out." Because sound cues are vital in helping children become fluent readers, this was a good cue for many words. It is not, of course, the only way to learn about words, and in many cases it is entirely ineffective. For example, while sounding out *basket* will likely give the new reader a good start on figuring it out, sounding out *breath* will only result in frustration. A student can sound out words that are phonetically regular—that is, where the letters make the sounds that students are taught they make and where there is generally one sound (as in consonants like *m*, *n*, *p*, and *k*), like *basket*, and where vowels follow the vowel rules, like *basket* or *snake*. Words that violate phonics rules—like *give*, which doesn't follow the silent -*e* rule, or like *city* (often decoded as *kitty*), which has letters with multiple sounds—or that appear before the student has been exposed to these rules, like *chair* before a child has learned the *ch* or *ai* blend, will not yield to this strategy (and there are many, many of them). Clearly, students need more strategies than only sounding a word out. Thus, teachers need ways to prompt students to invoke these strategies. Obviously, then, teachers need to be adept enough at thinking through these words and strategies so that they can decide whether "Sound it out" or "Think about the sounds" will be effective for a given word. Even in those cases where words are phonetically regular, teachers should also consider cues that are more specific than simply "Sound it out," such as covering up portions of the word, or finding the little word in the big word.

Clay (2006) talks about three kinds of cues that teachers offer when students struggle with word-level reading: meaning cues (semantic), structure cues (syntactic), and visual cues (graphophonic). Tompkins (2009) characterizes them similarly and also notes their overlap and interdependence in the word analysis strategies of readers. It is generally agreed that there can be a good deal of overlap, that there isn't always a single way to help a child figure out an unknown word, and that all children don't figure out all words in the same manner. We discuss each of these cueing systems in brief along with examples of words or situations that will or will not benefit from strategic attention to that category. Following, we offer another way of thinking about varied cues, that of skill-based or strategic cueing.

Meaning Cues

Meaning cues are those that rely on the context of the sentence. Using meaning cues is a practice very common in cueing older children who can decode a word but may not know the meaning of that word. Typically, a teacher might ask an older student to "use the context of the sentence" in a case such as the one below. The unknown word in the examples that follow in this chapter is printed in italics.

She *resembled* her mother in many ways, so much so that they were often mistaken for sisters.

A teacher cueing an older child might direct that child to the meaning of the end of the sentence in order to make a reasonable inference about the unknown word: *resembled*. The teacher might advise:

> "Think about what would make someone think that a mother and daughter were sisters. What do you think that would mean about their relationship to one another?"

The teacher might do this to show the student how to use meaning to try out reasonable definitions of words, a common upper elementary strategy for vocabulary learning.

Teachers of younger students can do the same by using meaning cues coupled with some phonological knowledge. Consider the following sentence where the student stumbles on the word *caught*.

Text reads: She *caught* the fish.
Student reads : She c, c, c. [Looks at teacher for assistance.]

A teacher might cue in the following manner:

> "Hm, why not read to the end of the sentence and see if you can figure anything out. Just skip the word you don't know, keep reading and try again."

For many students, getting to the word *fish* would be enough to prompt them to try out the word *caught* as many students will have had experiences reading or doing or hearing things that will help them infer the pronunciation of the word *caught*. If a child still isn't able to make an attempt at the word, the teacher might say:

> "Okay, let's think of the first sound of that word, /K/. Now that I know the first sound, let's read to the end of the sentence and see if we can guess at it."

This combination of an initial sound with the meaning of the rest of the sentence might be enough to get the child to make a reasonable inference about the pronunciation of the word. Whether the child gets the word in question or not, the point is that he or she begins to understand the idea of using meaning to figure out an unknown word.

Another way a teacher uses meaning cues is to show students how to insist, for themselves, that a sentence make sense. Consider the following example from a second-grade reader as he reads *Soccer Sam* by Jean Marzollo.

Text reads: Sam felt awful. "Let's go home," he told Marco.
Student reads: Sam felt above. "Let's go home." he told Marco.

Teachers familiar with miscue analysis will recognize the error as indicative of a lack of self-monitoring. Had the student been thinking through his own reading, checking his own understanding, he likely would have recognized that "above" was nonsensical in that context. Because he did not, and continued to read, a teacher can infer that his reading is such that it is interfering with comprehension or that he is unable to assign meaning to words as he reads this content. In either case, a meaning cue such as the following might help.

STUDENT: (*reading*) Sam felt above. "Let's go home." he told Marco.

TEACHER: I am going to stop you there. Can you read it again?

STUDENT: (*reading*) Sam felt above. "Let's go home." he told Marco.

TEACHER: I want you to be certain that as you read you think about what the words mean.

STUDENT: Okay.

TEACHER: So does it make sense to say "Sam felt above"? What does that mean? Remember that in a text such as this the sentences will make sense.

STUDENT: I guess it doesn't make sense but I don't know what word that is.

TEACHER: That is fine, don't worry about that word. Just remember the idea that if you read and find that something doesn't make sense that you probably have made a mistake somewhere. Okay?

STUDENT: Yes.

This teacher is strategic in suggesting to him that meaning is a criterion by which a student should judge whether or not his reading is coherent. More phrases that help teachers assist students in using meaning cues are in Figure 4.1.

Try again, this time take a running start . . .

Do you see a little word inside that big word that you might know?

Does this start/end like a word you do know?

What happens if I cover up this part, what do you see then?

Look at the picture, then the first sound, and see if you can guess.

What word might make sense there?

Does that look like a word on your word wall?

FIGURE 4.1. Common cues.

Structural Cues

Just as students sometimes infer meaning from semantic clues, they can infer meaning from clues about where the word rests in the sentence. Listen in on a conversation in a first-grade guided reading group.

Text reads: The boy is sad.

STUDENT: (*reading*) The boy is silly.

TEACHER: That is a great try. I see why you might think that word is *silly* since it starts with the /s/ sound and it makes perfect sense in that sentence.

The teacher might go on to direct the student to the ending sound of *sad* in order to get her to use other cues to decode this unknown word. The point is, though, this teacher can see that the student is aware of the kind of word that belongs in that position in the sentence, that she is using her syntactic knowledge of the way sentences function to approximate the word she cannot decode with automaticity. Had she substituted *sad* for a noun like *sun*, the teacher might have inferred a less elaborated syntactic understanding since a noun such as that would not belong placed in that sentence in that way.

Another use of syntactic knowledge is in the use of affixes such as *-s* or *-ed*. If a text reads "Jon sits in the chair" and a student decodes it as "Jon sit in the chair" he is displaying a lack of syntactic knowledge. This miscue is very common for English language learners and those who speak in various dialects, but unusual for native speakers without significant dialect in their natural talk.

Sound Cues

Sound or graphophonic cues are the most common and generally the most natural for teachers. The old stand-by, "Sound it out" is a very general phonological cue, one that we discourage for it rarely gives kids enough information to figure out an unknown word. There are other, more pointed cues, that should be considered because they offer graphophonic cues that are more helpful. Many teachers use rhymes, word families, and consonance to help students apply what they know about the sound of one word to an unknown word. Once students have the phonemic awareness to blend and segment words, they can use that skill to analyze words for their sounds and make a good inference about what it might be. Listen to two examples of teachers, the first working with a kindergartner late in the year, the second with a third grader.

Text reads: The cat is on the mat.

STUDENT: (*reading*) The cat is on the … ? (*Looks at teacher.*)

TEACHER: I see the word you are struggling with. Does it look like any of the other words in the sentence? What would happen if I covered these? (*Covers the /c/ in* cat *and the /m/ in* mat.) What do you notice?

STUDENT: Same letters.

TEACHER: Right. Now, you knew the first word was *cat*. Can you point to the /K/ sound and then to the /at/? (*Student is able to point to these parts.*) Now, let's try to point to parts of this other word and see if we can figure it out.

As you can see from this example, the teacher is drawing on what the student knows about the sounds in one word to apply them to the sounds in another. This is using phonological or sound cues to prompt accurate decoding. Here is an example from an older student who likely has a good deal of sound knowledge:

Text reads: The actual cost was much less.

STUDENT: (*reading*) The increased cost was much less.

TEACHER: That makes some sense, but I want you to go back and look at that second word. I am going to cover up the end. What is the beginning?

STUDENT: *Act.*

TEACHER: Right, so now try it again by rereading the whole sentence.

Notice in this example that following the cue, the teacher has the student go back and read the whole sentence so that she might use the context also now that she has a good start on the sounds. We encourage teachers to work on words with students and then embed them back in the sentence, thus having the student read the sentence correctly.

Using Cues in Combination

As you can see from these examples, cues often have components of each system. When a teacher asks a student to look at the first letter of a word, then a picture, then to try to guess the meaning, he or she is using elements of the phonological system as well as of the semantic and perhaps the syntactic systems as well. Knowing about the different systems can help broaden your arsenal of useful cues, but knowing which category of cue you are giving at any given time isn't necessary. Figure 4.1 gives a list of the most common cues that teachers use in responsive guided reading groups. Figure 4.2 gives you examples of exchanges in responsive guided reading groups. Figure 4.3 has some student miscues for you to practice and discuss with colleagues. There are often multiple possible cues for any one error, so don't discount your answer because it isn't the same as someone else's. There certainly are cues for some errors that won't be effective (e.g., having children sound out a phonetically irregular word, asking children to guess at a word using meaning cues when they don't know the meaning of the word), but there is also a range that might be effective. It is worth repeating that cueing is difficult, that it takes practice, and that teachers should expect to struggle in their first months of working in responsive guided reading groups.

MOVING ON TO THE NEXT STUDENT

Once a student has been cued, it is very often time to move on to the next student in the group. Even if there is still time left to spend with this student, a single cue can be more effective than a number of them. Before leaving the student, however, it is wise to help him or her to transfer the skill just scaffolded. We end the responsive guided reading group by saying something like:

> "Okay, now we learned that sometimes if you cover up parts of a word it helps you figure out what the word is. I want you, this week, to do that when you come to a word you don't know, at home, at school, wherever. Give it a try. If you are able to use that strategy, and it helps, be sure to come tell me."

This simple statement reminds the student that strategies aren't only something that you do in the company of the teacher, but something

Text reads: I want to go with you to the park.

ANDY: (*reading*) I like to go with you to the park.
TEACHER: What is this? (*Points to* want.)
ANDY: *Like.*
TEACHER: That is what you said. Check yourself, what does *like* start with?
ANDY: *L.*
TEACHER: Do you see an *L* in there?
ANDY: No.
TEACHER: What letters do you see?
ANDY: "Double *u.*"
TEACHER: What does a *W* say?
ANDY: /W/.
TEACHER: So if that word starts with a /W/ sound, let's try to read it again.

Text reads: Lamb has no mother.

MIA: (*reading*) Lamb heard on mother.
TEACHER: Does that make sense?
MIA: Lamb heard no mother.
TEACHER: (*Points to the word* has *and keeps her finger under it.*) Does that make sense?
MIA: Lamb has no mother.
TEACHER: Aha, now it makes sense.

Text reads: Inside the box was a fox.

JORDAN: (*reading*) Uh, uh, the box was a fox.
TEACHER: Hm.
JORDAN: I the box?
TEACHER: Hm, that is a hard word, but I bet we know parts of it. Do you see any little words in it that you know?
JORDAN: No.

FIGURE 4.2. Sample conversations.

(*continued*)

FIGURE 4.2. (*continued*)

TEACHER: Try covering up the end. (*Covers side.*)

JORDAN: *In.*

TEACHER: Now try.

JORDAN: *In, Inside* the box.

TEACHER: Great. You found the little word and it helped you with the big word.

Text reads: The girls and boys had to share their toys.

LEAH: (*reading*) The girls and boys had to sorry their toys.

TEACHER: Does that make sense? Remember, this text will always make sense.

LEAH: It doesn't make sense, really.

TEACHER: Let's look at that word. It is a hard word but I think you know a word that looks a lot like it. See if you see a word on the word wall that starts the same way as that word.

LEAH: *She?*

TEACHER: Right! What parts of *she* are also in that word?

LEAH: *Sh.*

TEACHER: Excellent. Now take a running start and see if you can get the word from that beginning sound.

Text reads: Every day he fights for a spot on the bus.

KYLE: (*reading*) Every day he.... (*Stops.*)

TEACHER: That is a hard word. It looks so different from any word we know. Try reading the sentence without it.

KYLE: Everyday he finds for a spot on the bus?

TEACHER: Great try. I like how you used the beginning sound to try it. The word is actually *fight*. We haven't talked about how *igh* sometimes sounds in words like *fight*, *night*, *light*. So the word is *fight*. Point to it and say it and then read the whole sentence.

KYLE: *Fight.*

TEACHER: Okay, now go on.

KYLE: Everyday he fights for a spot on the bus.

Text reads: But then the big dog came up and bit him.

Student reads: But the the big dog came up and bit him.

You say:

Text [accompanied by a picture of a boy blowing up a balloon] reads: He blew as hard as he ever had.

Student reads: He thought as hard as he ever had.

You say:

Text reads: The skate was new and white.

Student reads: The school was new and with.

You say:

FIGURE 4.3. Miscues to use for practice.

that can help when he or she is reading independently too. As discussed in Chapter 3, at the end of your work with each student you are going to ask him or her to repeat back to you the strategy that he or she worked on with you. You can then give another reminder to the whole group to be sure to look for opportunities to use the strategy and to tell you if they do. They may never remember to tell you, and the ideal is that they begin to incorporate these strategies automatically, but it is nice for them to know that you are there waiting for them should they wish to share their experience using the strategy.

RESOURCES FOR FURTHER READING

Cole, A. D. (2004). *When reading begins: The teacher's role in decoding, comprehension, and fluency.* Portsmouth, NH: Heinemann.

After many years of videotaped research, this author has concluded that there is a key to getting emergent readers reading: individualized scaffolding. She discusses exactly what teachers do and say, and what they *should* do and say, to help their young students develop into fluent readers.

Dorn, L., French, C., & Jones, T. (1998). *Apprenticeship in literacy: Transitions across reading and writing.* Portland, ME: Stenhouse.

The authors explain how to implement an apprenticeship approach to literacy in K–3 classrooms. Educators will learn how to support students in a balanced literacy program, and how to withdraw that support as students gain independence. A chapter on guided reading discusses emergent, early, and fluent guided reading.

Walpole, S., & McKenna, M. C. (2007). *Differentiated reading instruction: Strategies for the primary grades.* New York: Guilford Press.

These authors provide educators with strategies for differentiated reading instruction by devoting a chapter to each of the five essentials of primary reading: phonemic awareness, word recognition, fluency, vocabulary, and comprehension. They also provide differentiation plans for each grade level, K–3, that will help teachers begin the process of differentiation.

Wilde, S. (2000). *Miscue analysis made easy: Building on students' strengths.* Portsmouth, NH: Heinemann.

The author makes a case for using miscue analysis to identify students' reading strengths and then employing this information to support their further learning. The chapters offer information to help educators understand the reading process as well as the practice of miscue analysis. The author offers ideas for how to use miscue analysis as well as simplified versions of it within a progressive reading model.

Chapter 5

Prompting Fluent Readers during Responsive Guided Reading

*"I have watched my colleagues who teach
lower elementary students listen and respond
to miscues, but how do I tell what my older
readers need if they decode just fine?"*

Readers who are proficient decoders, both young ones and older students, benefit from the same kind of close attention to their reading as do those just learning to decode texts. We advocate using responsive guided reading groups all the way through the upper elementary grades with struggling, at-level, and advanced students. Many older students are capable decoders with abundant strategies for identifying unknown words, yet still they struggle to comprehend the text at hand. Harvey and Goudvis (2000) remind us that "reading involves both decoding and the making of meaning.... It involves cracking the alphabetic code to determine the words and thinking about those words to construct meaning" (p. 5). In order to be a skilled reader, students need to learn to decode as they also learn to construct meaning.

In Chapter 4, we discussed the way that responsive guided reading functions for beginning readers—as a place to work on word attack skills. We advocated working on meaning making for these developing readers in other contexts like read-alouds and shared reading. Once students no longer need such intense instruction in word recognition, they are ready to move to meaning making as the exclusive instructional focus of their reading education. It may be a surprise to many new teachers to learn that traditionally, once children were strong in word recognition, no formal reading instruction took place. Once students learned to read, they almost exclusively read to learn. This suggests that word recognition is the sole goal of reading instruction. It also discounts the importance of strategic reading instruction. Furthermore, it assumes that learning to read is a finite process. We believe that all students deserve reading instruction that helps them move to a higher level of skill and understanding. This includes fluent readers of all ages.

Rasinski (2003) defines *fluent readers* as those who "read quickly, effortlessly, and efficiently with good, meaningful expression" (p. 26). These fluent readers need different support for their reading than do those first learning to read. For young readers, responsive guided reading groups emphasize decoding so that students may become fluent enough to devote their cognitive resources to meaning making. Once this occurs, the emphasis shifts, yet the form remains the same. While teachers of younger children have always known that they can learn much about student strengths and weaknesses simply by listening to what they are able and not able to decode, teachers of older students have not always taken the opportunity to listen carefully to student out-loud reading to hear reading strengths and weaknesses. This may be, in part, because it isn't easy to note breakdowns in comprehension or vocabulary knowledge. As noted above, many students decode just fine but have no idea what they are reading. For teachers, one goal of responsive guided reading groups for fluent readers is to note when students read smoothly yet aren't making meaning from the text. Once teachers can recognize a breakdown in meaning making, they can provide cues to help students learn what to do when this happens during future reading. There are three broad areas that teachers work on with students in responsive guided reading groups once they are able decoders: comprehension, vocabulary, and fluency. Each of these is discussed briefly in the sections below. Following these sections we introduce a three-part structure that can help guide teachers as they work with fluent readers in responsive guided reading groups.

COMPREHENSION AND STANDARDS OF COHERENCE

It is helpful to understand what Grasser, McNamara, and Louwerse (2003) call "standards of coherence" when thinking about student comprehension breakdowns. These literacy experts contend that the overriding reason that students read without understanding is because they have a low standard of coherence. This means that they have low expectations for a text making meaning. When strong readers are confronted with a difficult text (and even the strongest readers will struggle with some texts), they expect that it will make sense. Their experience has shown them that all texts will make sense, eventually, or can make sense with the proper scaffolding, background knowledge, or strategic reading. Students, especially struggling students, have had many, many experiences with texts that do not make sense. Thus, they may read along quite contentedly saying every word either silently or aloud and never stop to consider that they haven't learned anything or assigned meaning to any of the words. For them, reading is often nonsensical, so this is nothing new. Their standard for coherence, for a text hanging together and making meaning, is low, so it isn't of particular surprise that the text at hand doesn't make sense. When skilled readers find that they have turned several pages and their thoughts have drifted elsewhere, they think to themselves (if they want or need to derive meaning from the text at hand) that they should do something: go back and reread, go back and try to ask questions of the text, look up some words, or something else from among their repertoire of things to do. Skilled readers realize that it is of no use to read words without attending to their meaning. Many students, however, believe that if they have decoded the words then they have completed their homework or required task, and they move on. A goal of comprehension instruction is getting students to self-monitor, to see that they aren't understanding, and to know a thing or two they might do about it. Therefore, when we think about responsive guided reading instruction for fluent readers, we might consider it as a way to raise their standard of coherence.

COMPREHENSION STRATEGY INSTRUCTION

Strategy instruction is widely thought of as the most potent form of comprehension learning (Duke & Pearson, 2002; Keene & Zimmerman, 2007; Pressley, 2000; Williams, 2002). When teachers work with a student or students to practice using comprehension strategies, they are offering a model for what a skilled reader might do when presented with a comprehension breakdown. Among the findings from *Reading for Understanding: Toward an R&D Program in Reading Comprehension* by the RAND Reading Study Group (2002) was that "the explicitness with which teachers teach comprehension strategies makes a difference in learner outcomes, especially for low-achieving students" (p. 33). "Strategy instruction" sounds fancy. Really, it is only the idea that students make meaning from difficult texts through an active, deliberate process that can be explicitly taught and then practiced. Readers who use strategies wisely learn to incorporate them into the way they read, always. Many students have some strategies that they use regularly even if they cannot articulate that they do. When readers are going through a text that is not difficult for them, they use strategies without knowing. This easy, comfortable reading (known as a student's independent reading level) should not be encumbered by explicit strategy use. Simply, if students can read and make meaning and don't know they are using a strategy to do so, or are not, so be it. Strategy instruction is therefore not helpful for students who are reading easy texts. It also isn't useful for students who are reading texts so difficult that they will never make meaning of them. These texts, considered frustration level, aren't appropriate for any reading instruction as they will merely aggravate students or make them believe their reading is not good. Strategy instruction is effectively practiced on instructional-level texts, texts that are just a bit too hard for students to understand unassisted or without explicitly invoking a strategy but within their range with one or both of these supports. (For more discussion of independent, instructional, and frustration levels, please see Chapter 10.)

The real point of strategy teaching is to urge students to self-monitor, to use metacognition (thinking about their thinking) to recognize a breakdown in understanding, and then to invoke a strategy and do something about it. This "something" can be as simple as rereading or as complex as outlining. Wise teachers explicitly teach, model, and guide students in the practice of a number of these strategies in the whole-group context. Students thus can use the responsive guided reading group to practice strategy instruction under the watchful, individualized eye of their teacher. This instructional method is similar to that for responsive guided reading groups focused on decoding in that a concept is introduced in the whole group and then practiced in responsive guided reading groups so that the instruction can be appropriately differentiated.

VOCABULARY LEARNING IN RESPONSIVE GUIDED READING GROUPS

Comprehension breaks down when students do not or cannot make meaning from texts. Often they do not make meaning because they aren't able to monitor the fact that they don't understand. Other times they are paying rapt attention but are unable to make the inferences necessary to make meaning. Still other times there are conceptual difficulties that create barriers. And sometimes it is the words themselves. A rich vocabulary is said to be the most indicative factor of school success (Stahl & Nagy, 2006). Nonetheless, many students come into school without exposure to the kinds of texts that increase vocabularies. There are also lots of students with rich vocabularies who read above their grade level and are hungry to grab onto the new, exciting words that appear in more sophisticated texts. While the responsive guided reading group is not the place where we introduce new words or word-learning strategies in any formal way, it is a place where a teacher has the opportunity to scaffold students as they encounter unknown words. When a teacher infers that a student's meaning making is hindered by a lack of word knowledge, the focus of the interaction in the responsive guided reading group might be a strategic approach to figuring out unknown words. Using word parts (Blachowicz & Fisher, 2009) and context clues (Kuhn & Stahl, 1998) are two among many strategic approaches to vocabulary learning that can be reinforced in the responsive guided reading group. Like comprehension strategies, these should be introduced, discussed, and practiced in a whole-group context and then reinforced in individual ways in the responsive guided reading group.

A WORD ABOUT FLUENCY

Reading quickly and with expression is not useful if meaning is not made. In this sense, fluency is never an end unto itself. Literacy researchers have shown a strong correlation between rate, speed, and understanding of text (National Institute of Child Health and Human Development, 2000). Nobody thinks that raw speed should be an exclusive goal, but studies with faster and slower readers suggest that those who move too slowly through a text struggle with comprehension. It is also true that those who read too quickly may struggle to make meaning. Teachers work hard to get kids reading smoothly and quickly enough so that their cognitive resources are freed for understanding. They also work hard to teach students that there is no valor in racing through a text such that comprehension suffers. In the responsive guided reading group, students read to the teacher for a very short time. Though this is surely not enough to exert any influence on their fluency, it is plenty of time for the teacher to hear the level of fluency a child has, and in many cases, to cue them to increase or decrease their pace depending on his or her assessment of the need.

CUES

Though we discussed fluency, comprehension, and vocabulary separately in the preceding sections, clearly they are intermingled in our reading practices. Readers can't comprehend if they don't have the vocabulary to do so. They can't comprehend if they aren't fluent enough to free their attention for meaning making. They won't be fluent if the vocabulary demands of a text are too high. Reading is not a discrete set of processes but a complex web of cognitive, social, and physical activities that overlap. In addition, the cognitive demands for the responsive guided reading teacher are significant and span three different parts. He or she must learn:

1. How to identify a possible breakdown in meaning making by listening to the student read (discussed in the section "Listening to Students Read").
2. How to check that the indication of meaning breakdown does in fact interfere with the child's reading understanding (discussed in the section "Determining If the Breakdown Has Occurred").
3. How to determine a cue that might help when the child is confronted with a similar situation in the future (discussed in the section "Cueing Students").

This three-part process—learning what to listen for, learning how to validate the hunch, and then learning what to say—is discussed below.

Listening to Students Read

Teachers of fluent readers often ask how they can determine if a student is comprehending based on his or her oral reading. It is easy to tell when a child cannot decode a word, yet as we have discussed earlier in this chapter, a reader may be perfectly adept at "word calling" without understanding a lick of what he or she has read. Our work with students and teachers in the upper elementary grades has helped us to identify some common indicators that a child's meaning is breaking down. These indicators don't always help us understand why; we discuss that issue following this section, but one thing at a time. Figure 5.1 offers a teacher "cheat sheet" to use when first working in responsive guided reading groups for fluent readers. This cheat sheet suggests what a teacher might initially listen for and might be helpful to use as you work with students as a reminder.

• *Fast pace.* When students read too quickly it is a good bet that they aren't attending to the meaning. Of course "fast" is relative, but a teacher who has been working with a student for a number of weeks will be able to determine if this is the child's usual pace. It isn't unusual for a student to read more quickly to the teacher in a responsive guided reading group because of the novelty, or for some kids, trepidation, of reading aloud with a teacher's full attention on him or her. For whatever the reason, this is a common indicator that a child is not carefully attending to meaning.

• *Monotone.* When readers make meaning during reading, they read with expression. This, sometimes referred to as prosody, is often the first indicator of a strong comprehender. Most often, when students are understanding, they vary their reading pace, their voice rises and falls, and the intonation of their vocalization changes word to word or sentence to sentence. It is true that some students are naturally less expressive or emotive in their oral reading, but again, a teacher familiar with the way a child reads will hear the difference between oral reading of something that the student is comprehending and oral reading where comprehension has broken down.

• *Reading through punctuation.* Readers who are not self-monitoring, that is, who are not checking their understanding, often read right through punctuation. They fail to pause at commas, to stop at periods, or to use intonations appropriate to question marks.

• *Mispronunciation.* When young readers decode a word inaccurately it often results in a nonsensical word or one that doesn't make sense in context. If they keep reading, that is, fail to self-correct, it is an indicator that they aren't making meaning from the text. This is the same with older students. When older students are confronted with unfamiliar words they may use the resources they remember from their earlier reading experiences (e.g., using sound cues, using context cues, using word parts). If what he or she arrives at doesn't make sense in the sentence, a reader who is appropriately making meaning will stop and try again. This lets us know that he or she is attempting meaning making and thus recognizing when it does not occur. Students who don't

Pace of reading
    Too fast
    Too slow

Expressions
    Present
    Absent

Pausing
    Stops at punctuation
    Doesn't stop at punctuation

Self-monitors
    Stops to correct
    Doesn't stop to correct

Body language
    Comfortable
    Not comfortable

FIGURE 5.1. Teacher cheat sheet: Clues that students may have a comprehension breakdown.

stop reading when something doesn't make sense often are not actively engaging in meaning making.

• *Reading too slowly.* When children read too slowly, they cannot keep all the information necessary in their heads to make meaning. The cognitive demands of word recognition may make real comprehension impossible as both compete for the reader's attention. It is not possible to comprehend without recognizing words, so that is the activity that occupies the first line of cognition (as well it should). When this is too significant a task, there can be no comprehension.

• *Observing body language.* Harvey and Goudvis (2000) remind us that sometimes a student's body posture, tics, or affect can teach us about his or her thinking. A furrowed eyebrow, a scrunched-up nose, or a hand over the mouth can all indicate discomfort that might suggest struggle.

Determining If the Breakdown Has Occurred

Sometimes student reading is consistent with one of the characteristics of comprehension breakdown discussed above, yet the student is indeed comprehending. Teachers will want to learn to listen for the descriptors of student reading discussed above to determine where they will stop students to see if they comprehend the text appropriately. There are many ways to determine this. Just like any instance where one wants to determine a reader's understanding, teachers can ask a literal or inferential question, they can ask students to summarize or retell that which was just read, they can ask them what the passage makes them think about, they can ask them to jot down the most important ideas, and so on. All of these techniques can help a teacher determine if indeed the reading behavior the teacher identified as likely indicating a meaning breakdown actually was a meaning breakdown. Teachers may want to experiment with each one of the above quick assessments to see which makes the most sense to them or provides them with the most information quickly. We want to make it clear that this is not an easy process. Learning how to probe a student's understanding can be complex. We recommend, again, having one or two ways that you repeatedly check for understanding rather than selecting from a number.

We find that the best solution is often the simplest. After the student reads a piece of a passage that we think the student does not understand we ask, "What just happened?" for a fiction text or "What information is being given here?" for a nonfiction text. Different ways to probe student understanding quickly, separated by fiction and informational texts, are summarized in Figure 5.2.

When the student cannot respond fully or appropriately, we take that as a sign that cueing is needed. If a student does respond accurately, we often say, "That is right, but something about the way you read it made me think you were having trouble understanding. Were you?" Though this may be difficult for students to answer, it is worth pursuing. They may say that they did have trouble understanding but made a good guess (not a bad strategy in itself); they may say they understood perfectly but were reading too slow or too fast or without expression for a reason. They may have no idea how to respond. In any case this becomes part of an ongoing conversation about reading.

Cueing Students

As you will remember from the beginning of this chapter, strong readers have a high standard of coherence. They expect texts to make sense and when they do not, they do something about it. When we work with readers in responsive guided reading groups, our goal is to get them to raise their standards of coherence, to stop reading and activate a strategy when they have trouble understanding. Though some students are painfully aware that they aren't understanding what they read, most read along without that awareness. Thus, many of the most common cues for fluent readers have to do with self-monitoring. At minimum we want students metacognitively equipped to understand that they aren't understanding. Our next goal, then, is to offer a number of strategies to try in order that they might better understand.

Fiction texts	Informational texts
What just happened?	What information is being discussed?
What do you predict will happen next and on what are you basing that prediction?	What did you just learn about X [bats, Helen Keller, the causes of the Civil War]
What other stories are like this one? In what ways?	What do you think the next section will cover?
Can you retell that passage?	Can you summarize the most important information?

FIGURE 5.2. Questions to ask to determine understanding.

When students don't understand what they read, it can be for one of two broad reasons. For some students the problem is attention. They are saying the words without activating the cognitive resources necessary to pay enough attention to what they are reading. This isn't always a matter of immaturity or not caring. For many students, they aren't able to engage with a text if it isn't inherently interesting to them. Other times, with other texts, students are attending but fail to comprehend nonetheless. This can be for any number of reasons. As you can see from Figure 5.3, these two kinds of meaning breakdown require different responses.

Cueing to Attend

Many comprehension weaknesses derive from students reading without activating the processes that will help them assign meaning to words or passages. All of us have the experience of disengaging from a text, continuing to move through it, and then realizing we haven't comprehended at all. As we discussed earlier, good readers will not accept that as a valid reading and will either decide not to pursue the text (if they have that choice, as in pleasure or self-selected reading) or will return to it with renewed dedication to meaning making. If students are not attending to the text, they will likely exhibit some of the behaviors described above: monotone, too fast or too slow, reading through punctuation. When they query students, teachers will see if students are not understanding fully and can provide a number of scaffolds. Since the idea is to help students to attend, we sometimes frame it as the teacher in the example below does.

TEACHER: What do you think the most important part of that passage was?

STUDENT: I'm not sure. I am not really sure.

TEACHER: You know what I do when I am reading along and I realize I am not sure I am getting enough out of it? I go back and read it again to be sure I was giving it my full attention. Let's have you try that.

1. Student didn't attend.	Teacher uses attending cues.
2. Student attended but didn't understand.	Teacher uses meaning cues.

FIGURE 5.3. Two kinds of cues to use when students don't comprehend what they read.

Another teacher reminds a student of what they have previously discussed in whole-class instruction:

TEACHER: That sounded strange. What do you think will happen next?
STUDENT: I think he will, I mean … go?
TEACHER: Go where?
STUDENT: (*Shrugs.*)
Teacher: Do you remember what we talked about the other day? That sometimes it is hard to pay attention and one way to do that is to try to think about what will happen next as you read? Remember practicing that with our textbooks? Let's have you go back and reread and try it here.

You will notice that the first teacher cues the student by telling him what she does when she is confronted with a similar struggle. Her hope is that with enough repetition he will incorporate this strategy and use it independently. The second teacher reinforces a strategy already among the student's repertoire. Both of these help students to move toward reading independence by allowing the teacher to scaffold their reading. Listed below are some common cues.

• *Go back and reread.* When students aren't attending they need to be directed to do so. Sometimes this is as easy as saying, after the student has shown an inability to comprehend that which was read, Why not go back and reread? If the text is within their capacity, this may be all they need.

• *Go back, reread and ask, image, connect.* Sometimes just going back and rereading is not enough to get students to attend. Teachers might direct students to practice one of the strategies discussed in class when they are rereading. Teachers might also have students stop after every sentence and think aloud to help them to use the strategy deliberately. For example:

"I want you to go back and try reading again. This time, though, I want you to stop here [points halfway through] and ask a question, any question that pops in your head when you read."

By asking the student to do something, the teacher is forcing the student to slow down, monitor, and act on his or her reading.

• *Go back and read more slowly, stop deliberately at the punctuation, try to speed up, use expression.* If a teacher believes that student fluency is suffering because he or she is not attending, it is often wise to have him or her read again, paying attention to something about pace, cadence, or expression. This is sometimes enough to help students engage with the text. For example:

> "You know you read that in such a flat tone. Can you go back and read it to me with some expression?"

Meaning Cues

The above are the "attending to text" strategies. There is also another category of cues that scaffold strategies related to a student's inability to understand because of conceptual issues, vocabulary weaknesses, or deficits in background knowledge. When these are the problems, it isn't that students haven't attended; it is that even with all their attention they still can't quite get it. When this happens, it is usually noted because students reread using the cues given above and still cannot succeed. These weaknesses call for different kinds of strategic cues, ones we call "meaning cues."

Meaning cues are those that help students to understand what they are reading. When students are weak in vocabulary, background knowledge, or experience with difficult concepts, all the self-monitoring in the world will not help them gather meaning from the text. This is where strategy instruction has been so effective. Pressley (2000) states that "active meaning instruction that occurs when students are explicitly taught to use and articulate comprehension strategies when they read" (p. 554) is the goal of instruction for fluent readers. Many teachers are familiar with this thinking about the value of strategy instruction. For further reading on this subject, see, for example, Harvey and Goudvis (2007) and Keene and Zimmerman (2007). In whole-class comprehension strategy discussion like that presented in the Duffy (1997) model, teachers introduce strategies through cognitive modeling or thinking aloud as they read to the whole group. Students are then lead through guided practice using the modeled strategy and over time move toward independent use.

These are the strategies that we encourage teachers to emphasize in a responsive guided reading group when student reading reveals that despite attention paid, the student is still struggling to make meaning. The particular strategies that a teacher will emphasize depend on the demands of the particular text and on the strategies that have been previously discussed and practiced in class. The responsive guided reading group is not a context where new strategies are presented, but instead one where familiar strategies are cued when a teacher notes they may assist a student in reading. Following are three common comprehension strategies and examples of how teachers prompt students to use them during responsive guided reading. One of the strategies, summary, is appropriate for informational texts. The other two, making connections and asking questions, are appropriate for informational or fiction texts. Following these examples is an instance of a teacher prompting a vocabulary strategy as the teacher inferred from the student reading that it was a lack of word understanding that led to the difficulty.

Summarizing. Asking a student to stop and summarize a passage is one way to determine if he or she is able to make meaning out of the text. It is also a tool for doing so. When a student cannot summarize, one way to help is to ask him or her to reread the text and summarize smaller portions. Often reading suffers because the student is overwhelmed by too much information at once. Breaking it down and having students stop and organize it for themselves can be of great benefit. Here is an example of a teacher who uses summarizing to determine a meaning breakdown and then prompts a student to summarize in order to help her make meaning of a difficult passage:

TEACHER: Can you tell me what you think the main points of that passage might be?

STUDENT: I am not really sure. I don't really understand.

TEACHER: Okay, let's go back and reread and see if we can stop after each couple of sentences and figure out what of importance was said. Then, at the end, we will see if we can bring it all together.

Connecting. Connecting a difficult text with life experiences, other texts, or previous knowledge can help students with conceptual difficulties. Sometimes it serves to remind students of something they forgot they knew; other times it brings up ideas that lead to new ideas. Many teachers instruct students in making text-to-self, text-to-text, or text-to-life connections. These can be practiced in the responsive guided reading group as shown below:

TEACHER: Okay, now that we see that this was hard, let's stop and go back and try to think about what this makes us think about. Do you know anything about the West?

STUDENT: I visited California with my parents. Oh, yeah, and I read a book about a kid in the Gold Rush.

TEACHER: So what are some specific memories you have of the climate when you visited California? Maybe that has implications for the growing of crops. Another thing to think about is what you might have learned about the crops from reading the book you mentioned. Now when you reread let's try to call those into our mind and see if they help you understand what they are saying about the problems with those kinds of crops growing in the western states.

Questioning. Asking questions of the text is another way to engage fully so that meaning might be constructed. The kind of question, and if it is answerable, isn't nearly as important as the act of thinking through what to ask. A student does that with his teacher in the next example:

TEACHER: Try stopping after this part and asking a question, anything you might want to know about the character and why she is acting that way.

STUDENT: Okay. (*reading*) "She never, ever wanted to see that teacher again, yet here she was back for another year of torture. She put her head down on the desk and cried." I don't really get who was crying, the girl or the teacher. Who is crying?

TEACHER: Great question. Let's see if we can figure it out.

Vocabulary Strategy. If the teacher has a hunch that the meaning breakdown is at a word level, that there are just too many unknown words, or even just a few that have effect on meaning, cues sound a little bit different. For this aspect of reading, teachers help students invoke vocabulary strategies that they have discussed and practiced in class. Here are some ways teachers encourage the practice of vocabulary strategies:

"That is a hard word, isn't it? Why not guess at what you think it means and then see if that makes sense in the sentence?"

"I bet you know part of that word. Look at just the beginning. What does that remind you of?"

"That word is very hard. What is something we can do if we come to a word we don't know?"

In Their Pockets

Regardless of the reason for the error and the cue given, it is important to remind students that the purpose of a responsive guided reading group is to develop strategies that can be used when students' meaning making suffers as they read independently. As we do for younger students, we remind our students to use what they practiced with the teacher as they read across the content areas, when they are working in their literacy block, and at home. The last thing a teacher might say is:

> "Okay, now next time you come to something that is hard to understand, try to do what we did together today. It won't always work, but getting into the habit of trying something when meaning breaks down is always a good thing to do."

RESOURCES FOR FURTHER READING

Fountas, I. C., & Pinnell, G. S. (2001). *Guiding readers and writers, grades 3–6: Teaching comprehension, genre, and content literacy.* Portsmouth, NH: Heinemann.

This book will help upper elementary teachers implement an effective guided reading program. It provides detailed information on understanding guided reading, grouping, and using leveled texts. Each chapter gives specific strategies for teaching struggling readers. Features include a comprehensive list of 1,000 books organized by title and level as well as numerous forms, graphic organizers, lists, and bibliographies.

Harvey, S., & Goudvis, A. (2007). *Strategies that work: Teaching comprehension for understanding and engagement* (2nd ed.). York, ME: Stenhouse.

This second edition shows educators how to teach comprehension strategies explicitly across the curriculum. It is filled with specific, easy-to-follow lesson plans such as "Linking What We Know to What We Learn" and "Paraphrasing to Summarize Expository Text." Useful items in the appendices include lists of great books to teach comprehension strategies and anchor charts for the comprehension strategies.

Keene, E. O. (2007). *Assessing comprehension thinking strategies.* Huntington Beach, CA: Shell Education.

This extensive reading comprehension assessment tool examines *how* students think when they read. The assessments cover strategies such as using schemas, determining importance in a text, and monitoring comprehension. These assessments can be given one on one, in a small group, and either in an oral or a written format.

Keene, E. O., & Zimmermann, S. (2007). *Mosaic of thought: The power of compre-hension strategy instruction* (2nd ed.). Portsmouth, NH: Heinemann.

This second edition explicitly describes the use and benefits of strategy-based comprehension instruction. It will help teachers implement practical, thoughtful ideas for teaching key comprehension strategies: monitoring com-prehension, using schemas, questioning, inferring, sensory imaging, determin-ing importance, and synthesizing. There is also a chapter that includes a section of frequently asked questions about strategy-based comprehension instruc-tion.

McLaughlin, M., & Allen, M. B. (2001). *Guided comprehension: A teaching model for grades 3–8*. Newark, DE: International Reading Association.

The authors provide a systematic teaching framework called the guided comprehension model that is designed to help students and teachers experi-ence reading as a thinking process. This model encourages students to become active, strategic readers by providing direct strategy instruction, numerous opportunities for engagement, and a variety of texts and instructional settings. The appendix is filled with helpful reproducibles such as forms for organiz-ing and managing comprehension centers and routines, literature response prompts, assessment forms, and leveled book resources.

Miller, D. (2002). *Reading with meaning: Reading comprehension in the primary grades*. York, ME: Stenhouse.

Intended for teachers of primary classrooms, this book addresses the same seven key comprehension strategies that Keene and Zimmermann's *Mosaic of Thought* addresses. Chapters include sections on anchor lessons and evidence of independence and understanding. It contains many examples of authentic student work that demonstrate the comprehension strategies in action.

Part III

Getting Started with Responsive Guided Reading

Practical Considerations

Chapter 6

The First Month of School
Establishing Routines

"My students do really well when they are in the groups with me. It is the rest *of the students who cannot handle it. They are bouncing off the walls while I am trying to run a group. Short of having another adult in the classroom— which won't happen—what can I do?"*

The teachers with whom we work believe in guided reading. They want to listen to students read, they want to differentiate their instruction based on student needs, and they want to use these opportunities for formative assessment to inform their instruction. Listening to students read individually is among our most potent diagnostic tools. When teachers listen carefully to students, the information they gain is as pure as possible: no writing confounds the impressions, no other students complicate the interaction. The child reads, the teacher listens. In addition, this activity is efficient for both parties in accomplishing key goals: the teacher gathers information on the child's strengths and weaknesses, the child feels fully heard and can get customized cueing, the kind of cueing only available one on one.

Teachers wish to use guided reading as an important component of their literacy block, but many don't or do so in only very limited ways. Literacy coaches with whom we work say that teachers new to guided reading are often paralyzed by the prospect of organizing the remainder of the class so that these students can work independently

while the teacher meets with small groups. It is of interest to us that we
hear this from teachers of the very youngest pupils and from those who
work with upper elementary children. It may be of interest to these
teachers that we have seen children beautifully engaged in authentic,
independent work at all grade levels including kindergarten. We know
that students can do this. We also know that it isn't intuitive for all or
even most students; thus, they need careful instruction in what to do
and how to do it.

Because of the intensity and, at times, difficulty of cueing students based on their struggles, teachers must be able to fully concentrate on the task at hand. Their full attention must be focused on the
students in the responsive guided reading group; they cannot be pre-
occupied with managing the rest of the students or worrying that students are not using their time wisely. Thus, the careful arrangement
and organization of independent student work is key to the success
of the groups.

This chapter focuses on getting students ready for their role as
independent workers during the time that their teacher is running the
guided reading group. Making students feel as if they are part of the
success of the group, whether or not they are in the group, may promote their complicity and cooperation. When teachers set the stage for
working with students on their behaviors relative to independent work
during guided reading, they make it clear that everyone's success in
improving their reading is reliant upon good, productive use of independent literacy work time.

As you recall from Chapter 2, guided reading time, when the
teacher is involved in instruction with one small group of children at
a stretch, is coupled with independent literacy work time. We define
responsive guided reading as the participation of a teacher and a small
group of students in small-group activities. We define *independent literacy work time* as the activities of the rest of the class during responsive
guided reading. For the purposes of this book, we include the activities
of the rest of the class as part of the success or struggles for teachers as
they implement guided reading. The most skilled reading teacher in
the world will not be able to teach a handful of children if the rest of the
class is out of control. When all goes as it should, the other children are
working on fruitful literacy activities that they can manage without an
adult present.

For some teachers, this fruitful literacy work will take the form of
literacy centers: distinct, often differentiated activities that children can

do individually, in pairs, or as part of a self-functioning small group. During this time, students will work in one center for a designated amount of time—say 15 minutes or so—about the amount of time of a single guided reading group. After the time elapses, students often switch to another center, ultimately visiting each center in the space of a few days or a week.

For other teachers, it is more comfortable to have the entire class engaging in the same activity at the same time, though often with materials that are differentiated for performance levels. In our view, teachers should select tasks that are worthwhile and can be done without teacher intervention. These can be in centers or not. Teachers should decide for themselves how much collaboration and movement they believe their students can manage and still remain productive workers.

Whatever form the teacher selects, telling the students to do it and expecting them to master behavior control, fulfill task demands, and troubleshoot problems without careful preparation is a sure recipe for failure. The remainder of this chapter explains the process of establishing routines for independent literacy work during the first month of school. This month prepares students for the behaviors and cognitive tasks that are required for a successful guided reading period whether students are moving through centers or engaging in independent literacy work at their desks. Though some teachers rankle at the idea that they will delay doing guided reading groups until 4 weeks into the school year, those who have taken shortcuts or skipped key components of this process in order to more hastily begin have most often regretted that decision. Once students fully understand the routines and procedures, the guided reading/independent literacy work time goes quite smoothly and this smooth work time can last for the entire year—less a tune-up or two, which we discuss later in this chapter. It is also reassuring to know that teachers who work in buildings where preparing students for guided reading is the norm may find that students who have been prepared for this in early grades need less time to adjust in the older grades. For now, let's look at the way that students—little and big—can be prepared to best ensure success and classroom harmony even when the teacher's attention is directed to only a few children.

To begin, Figure 6.1 shows a model calendar that covers the components of what we call "the guided reading training month" and where they might be housed in these beginning days of school. You can see that this schedule lists "center 1," "center 2," and so on. Even teachers who aren't planning to use centers need to teach students what

Monday	Tuesday	Wednesday	Thursday	Friday
Independent reading base Center 1 explanation	Independent reading base Center 1 procedures	Independent reading base Center 1 practice	Independent reading base Center 2 explanation	Independent reading base Center 2 procedures
Independent reading (base + 2 minutes) Center 2 practice	Independent reading (base + 2 minutes) Center 3 explanation	Independent reading (base + 2 minutes) Center 3 procedures	Independent reading (base + 2 minutes) Center 3 practice	Independent reading (base + 2 minutes) Practice: Three centers at once
Independent reading (base + 4 minutes) Center 4 explanation	Independent reading (base + 4 minutes) Center 4 procedures	Independent reading (base + 4 minutes) Center 4 practice	Independent reading (base + 4 minutes) Guided reading group practices (silent or whisper reading)	Independent reading (base + 4 minutes) Guided reading group practices (silent or whisper reading)
Independent reading (base + 6 minutes) Guided reading group practices (waiting)	Independent reading (base + 6 minutes) Guided reading group practices (waiting)	Independent reading (base + 6 minutes) Guided reading plus centers in real time	Independent reading (base + 6 minutes) Guided reading plus centers in real time	Independent reading (base + 6 minutes) Guided reading plus centers in real time

FIGURE 6.1. Planning template: Training month for guided reading processes.

to do when they are working in groups with other students. For the purpose of this chart, we refer to these as centers. A further explanation follows.

This month is largely devoted to helping children function in this special part of the literacy block. However, we urge teachers to prepare students in similar ways for other activities they will engage in as they learn to read and write. Because we are focusing on guided reading in this book, we have included the schedule only for those components that affect the success of the guided reading/independent literacy work period. When we work with teachers on their entire literacy block, this schedule has many more components.

BUILDING A BASE

For almost all teachers, independent reading of self-selected books is an important part of the independent literacy work period. Some teachers treat this as a center. The children who are engaged in that center, then, would be reading self-selected books, perhaps followed by some kind of written response, perhaps not. Other teachers have the entire class doing independent reading for a portion of the guided reading group; some, in fact, do this for the entire session. Whatever role independent reading of self-selected texts plays, students need to be carefully prepared for doing so. Atwell (1998) notes that for some students, the simple act of reading self-selected texts is not so simple. She believes that teachers ought to spend some time "building stamina" for independent reading, that is, increasing the time children are able to concentrate on independent reading. It is indeed true that in a given class there are many children who can engage in independent reading of a pleasurable book almost indefinitely. For these children, there is no need to build stamina. Other children become restless after a very short time even if the text they are reading is appealing to them. For independent reading time to be successful, it is important that all children are engaged in independent reading, not only those for whom the time flies effortlessly. The first month of school is the ideal time to begin to build capacity as a class, capacity for sustained engagement in silent reading.

In order to ensure the productivity of everyone during independent reading, every child must be taught to be productively engaged. For many teachers this begins in the following manner: On one of the first days of school the teacher asks students to pick a book from the classroom library that is appealing to them, or she assigns students "homework" to bring in a book from home that they love and look forward to reading either again or for the first time. Younger students should be encouraged to select picture books, older students fiction texts, periodicals, comic books, or anything else that they are looking forward to reading. A third option is to ask the librarian or media specialist to bring in a number of high-interest texts that he or she can book-talk or "advertise" to students and that can be left in the classroom for a period of days. Whatever way you get there, it is imperative that each student have a text (or for younger students, multiple texts) of their own choice.

Once all students have texts, the teacher describes what students should do if they find, a few minutes or more into the session, that they do not like the book. We have all had the experience of thinking something was going to be enjoyable and finding that it is not. The point of this activity is not to get students to continue to read something that is difficult or that they don't like, but to show students that reading independently can and should be engaging and pleasant. There may be times in the literacy curriculum to teach kids to push through texts that bore them or are difficult, but this is not the time. Because of this, English language learners should be encouraged to bring in books in their native language if that is the language in which it is easier for them to read. Special needs students who have an individual aide may listen to that adult read quietly to them if their disability is such that this is necessary.

In order to help students find enjoyable texts, some teachers keep a collection of student-friendly books and magazines with engaging text and pictures (e.g., *Sports Illustrated Kids, National Geographic Kids, American Girl*, comic books, *Time for Kids*, joke books, *Highlights*, or *Nick Magazine*) that they encourage students to select if their original choice proves to be disappointing. Other teachers direct students back to the classroom library to make another selection. Still others encourage their students to have a collection of books with them during independent reading, so that they can easily and quickly find another book. The point is to have a previously understood protocol for managing students who don't like their text. We don't want students struggling to read during this time. We want them to engage and enjoy.

Once these procedures have been set up and, in many cases, modeled and practiced, the teacher asks students to begin reading and starts a timer. He or she carefully monitors the class until he or she notes more than one or two students appear to disengage from their reading. Acknowledging that there are some students whose cognitive or social disabilities make it such that sitting still is nearly impossible, the teacher makes a reasonable inference about how long most of the kids are managing to read without much squirming. He or she marks down the time and this becomes the "class base," that is, the amount of time the teacher believes almost all students can engage productively in independent reading without management or adult oversight and redirection. Recall that students will likely be asked to engage in independent reading while the teacher is busy with a small group, and so they need to function well on their own. Though the teacher knows that many of the students could go on much longer, for the purposes of this activity he or she is interested in the amount of time that he or she can be certain *everyone* is quietly reading. The time may be very short—even 2 or 3 minutes for younger children or students who haven't spent much time reading for pleasure. It may be much longer—up to 15 or 20 minutes in the rare cases that may involve small classes or unusually focused readers. No matter what the base, the goal is to increase it, to build stamina in the way that athletes learn to run a short distance and then add little by little to get to their ultimate goal. It is reasonable to expect that in most classes, students can increase this by about 2 minutes or more per week for a 6-minute (and often more) increase by the end of the first month. This new number can then be used as teachers plan the way their students will spend time while they are working in small responsive guided reading groups. It isn't wise to ask students to read independently for 20 minutes if all of them cannot do it, because the students who cannot do it will become distracted and likely distract even those who can. Consider the case of a third-grade teacher, Ms. Latten.

Ms. Latten determines, using the method above, that her students, all of them, can read productively for about 8 minutes on the second day of school. For the remainder of that first week, then, she has them read for just that amount of time and then stops them. When they have proven a few times in a row that this is a realistic amount of time for everyone to stay on task, she lets them know that she is going to increase the time (just like athletes, she tells them, who run a mile and then a little more and then a little more, or start with 50 push-ups and increase at intervals until they are up to 100) a bit. For the second week, then, the students read silently for 10 minutes. When Ms. Latten is satisfied that her students can do this with success, she increases it yet again through the remaining weeks of this first month.

Since most responsive guided reading groups last 15 minutes, it isn't necessary (for these purposes) to increase the time by much more than that though some teachers, especially upper-elementary teachers, may very well continue to increase the time throughout the year. The sample schedule in Figure 6.1 shows one example of periodic increases in the course of the first month of school.

OTHER INDEPENDENT LITERACY ACTIVITIES

Chapter 7 discusses productive literacy activities that will engage students while the teacher is working with small groups. In this chapter, we discuss the ways in which effective teachers prepare students to function independently and productively by wisely using the first month of school to teach procedures and routines. Above we discussed one such productive activity, independent reading of self-selected texts, but as you will read in Chapter 7, there are many others. No matter which activities you select, you will want to feel confident that students can manage themselves; and they can, with sufficient time spent on building routines and understanding procedures.

Commonly, as discussed earlier, teachers pair guided reading time with either centers or independent literacy activities. There is no magic to either of these: the decision rests upon teacher preference and student capability. Either can and will work given careful setup.

When teachers elect to use centers they design differentiated literacy activities that students move through in small groups. Often these groups are the same as their guided reading groups. In a class of 30 students, there may be up to six guided reading groups. At any given time, one of the groups is working with the teacher, so the teacher provides up to five centers. It isn't necessary that these all be different. More than one group can work in one center at a time as long as materials can be shared. Thus, each guided reading group begins the day in one or another center, works through it for some amount of time (generally the amount of time it takes the teacher to work with one group), and then moves to another and sometimes another. Figure 6.2 is an example of the first 3 days of the week in centers. Thursday repeats Monday and Friday repeats Tuesday. Groups 1 and 2, the groups with the most struggling students, meet with the teacher twice in a week. If a class is smaller, this schedule can be adjusted to accommodate only five groups.

MONDAY	Group 1	Group 2	Group 3	Group 4	Group 5	Group 6
Session 1	Guided reading	Independent reading	Independent writing	Buddy reading	Research center	Word work
Session 2	Word work	Guided reading	Independent reading	Independent writing	Buddy reading	Research center
TUESDAY	Group 1	Group 2	Group 3	Group 4	Group 5	Group 6
Session 1	Research center	Word work	Guided reading	Independent reading	Independent writing	Buddy reading
Session 2	Buddy reading	Research center	Word work	Guided reading	Independent reading	Independent writing
WEDNESDAY	Group 1	Group 2	Group 3	Group 4	Group 5	Group 6
Session 1	Independent writing	Buddy reading	Research center	Word work	Guided reading	Independent reading
Session 2	Independent reading	Independent writing	Buddy reading	Research center	Word work	Guided reading

FIGURE 6.2. Schedule for responsive guided reading groups and independent literacy activities.

The teacher may prefer, for the sake of simplicity, that all children are working on the same literacy activity (yet often with differentiated materials). In this model, the shift happens day by day. For example, using the centers activities above, this classroom would run as such. On Monday Session 1, Group 1 would be with the teacher working in a guided reading group. Groups 2, 3, 4, 5, and 6 would all be doing independent reading. On Monday Session 2, Group 2 would be with the teacher working in a guided reading group. Groups 1, 3, 4, 5, and 6 would all be doing independent reading. A sample weekly schedule is shown in Figure 6.3.

In the first model each individual group might be working in one center, then they would switch. In the second model, Monday might be independent reading for all students, Tuesday might be word work for all students, Wednesday might be independent writing for all students, and so on. Some teachers might also elect to have students do two activities, one during the first guided reading group and another during the second. This option works well for students who will have difficulty concentrating on a single task for two 15-minute periods. The two approaches vary only in the way students move through them. The distinctions just discussed are summarized in Table 6.1.

PREPARING CHILDREN FOR CENTERS AND INDEPENDENT LITERACY WORK

No matter which configuration works best for you and your students, you'll need to spend a good amount of time during the first month of school getting them ready. As shown in the training month schedule, we believe it is best to attend to one activity at a time, introduce it, model both desirable and undesirable behaviors, have students practice with ample feedback from you, and continue this practice until you believe that all students can be successful. Often teachers do model behaviors

TABLE 6.1. Literacy Centers versus Daily Independent Literacy Work

Literacy centers	Daily independent literacy work
Small groups rotate activities.	Entire group does same activity.
Centers stay the same all week (or longer).	Group does different activity each day.
Students often move physically.	Students usually do not move far from their desks.

	Monday		Tuesday		Wednesday		Thursday		Friday (repeats Monday)
Group 1	Guided reading	Independent reading	Word work		Independent writing		Guided reading	Buddy reading	
Group 2	Independent reading	Guided reading	Word work		Independent writing		Buddy reading	Guided reading	
Group 3	Independent reading		Guided reading	Word work	Independent writing		Buddy reading		
Group 4	Independent reading		Word work	Guided reading	Independent writing		Buddy reading		
Group 5	Independent reading		Word work		Guided reading	Independent writing	Buddy reading		
Group 6	Independent reading		Word work		Independent writing	Guided reading	Buddy reading		

FIGURE 6.3. Schedule for independent activities.

and procedures but then don't give students time to practice and make mistakes before the actual behavior is needed. Each activity should be introduced and discussed on one day using an anchor chart (Boushey & Moser, 2006) of desirable and undesirable behaviors, modeled on another, practiced with feedback, and then practiced again until there is no mistaking what students are expected to do. Many teachers find if they list out all the components of the activity it helps them keep from overlooking what might be an important component. One such list, for the independent literacy activity of "buddy reading," is in Figure 6.4. In the buddy reading center, children select a pleasurable book and read it with a classmate. Students take turns reading to one another and often follow with a joint project or written response. As you can see, there are multiple steps to this seemingly simple activity. Some of these take just a minute to teach students to do and others might take multiple days. Nothing is too simple to model and discuss in preparation for students' engaging in this activity on their own.

This procedure would continue for each independent literacy activity regardless of whether students will be doing them in centers or all together on the same day. Figure 6.5 is a model schedule for teaching students how to function, without teacher direction, during buddy reading.

EASE INTO IT

There is no reason that teachers have to drive themselves crazy teaching five different independent literacy activities or centers. It is perfectly

---

- Determine who their buddy is.
- Find the place in the room designated for buddy reading.
- Learn to select books for buddy reading.
- Learn what to do if the selection proves problematic (too hard, too easy, dull).
- Learn to sit next to one another and read together (students need to learn what to do when they are the reader and what to do when they are the listener).
- Learn to record their buddy reading books in buddy reading journal.
- Learn how to troubleshoot when a buddy misbehaves.

FIGURE 6.4. Things students need to learn to do to prepare for buddy reading.

Monday	Tuesday	Wednesday	Thursday	Friday
Introduce idea. Use interactive writing to arrive at anchor chart of desirable and undesirable behaviors.	Go through procedure step by step. Borrow an extra adult for 10 minutes to buddy up and model an actual interaction. Show a video of students doing buddy reading if you can locate one.	Have students practice as you wander around and coach. Debrief activity.	Same as Wednesday.	Same as Wednesday.

FIGURE 6.5. Schedule for teaching buddy reading.

reasonable to teach students two or three and have them repeat them more than once in a week. It is much wiser to teach students to do a few things well than to try and do more for the sake of variety. If teachers decide to use the option of centers, they should also be sure to build in time to teach students how to physically move from center to center.

GUIDED READING PRACTICE

Because the teacher runs the responsive guided reading group, the need to practice in order to ensure independent behavior is unnecessary. What is necessary is instruction in some of the cognitive demands of the group so that the teacher need not stop the groups—once they get going—to help children learn these sometimes difficult activities. Chief among the things to learn is how to read quietly when other students are reading to the teacher. Younger students will need to be instructed in whisper reading (reading aloud but under their breath) and older ones in silent reading (or reading in my head) to keep the groups as quiet as possible so the teacher may focus on one child at a time. Another important skill is to help students think about what to do if they finish the text at hand or if it is so difficult for them that they simply cannot continue. Recall from the discussion in Chapter 1 that the teacher selects a book that is too hard for the students in order to force them to miscue or have a comprehension breakdown so that he or she might cue them in the moment. While the teacher works with one student, for a very short time, the other students are reading the book at a whisper or silently as best they can. For very young children where few words are on a page, they may finish before the teacher arrives. For older ones, they may find the activity too hard on any given day. Either way, a set procedure to minimize the squirming and off-task behavior typical when students believe they don't have anything to do is necessary. One note to teachers about this: we have seen plenty of students put their books down and listen to the other student read to the teacher and the teacher instruct that student. We see this as a fine strategy for students who are so distracted they cannot read while hearing others or who finish quickly. We don't think that there is anything wrong with one student overhearing another student working with the teacher. If this keeps him or her quiet and engaged, it might be encouraged. Generally, though, teachers instruct children to read the text again, to do a short written or picture response, to do some highlighting, or to do anything that will keep them from distracting others (the teacher included) in the close confines of this small-group work.

Some of this discussion and practice will likely be done as a whole class. For instance, everyone needs to learn to whisper read and to try to block out others reading near them. This takes experience. Students will improve as the year goes on. The mark of a teacher who consistently does guided reading groups is that most students are not bothered by others reading aloud to the teacher in their vicinity. Everyone also needs to know what to do in the cases discussed above, when for whatever reason they are not reading. This instruction won't take nearly as long as instruction in the independent literacy centers, however, as the presence of the teacher tends to act as a powerful reminder to behave as expected.

BRINGING IT ALL TOGETHER

Once students have had instruction in independent literacy activities and in guided reading group procedures, it is time to practice these together in real time. During the last week or so of this training month, the teacher pulls groups as he or she will do once the actual events begin and the rest of the class engages in independent literacy activities on their own. The purpose of this is to monitor their ability to function independently. If they cannot, the teacher knows more instruction is in order. This "simulation" should be done for as long as the teacher plans to spend with actual responsive guided reading groups. It is worth repeating that there is no reason to move to the next stage (conducting responsive guided reading groups) if the students cannot yet function as the teacher needs them to function. It may seem long, it may even seem redundant, yet it is absolutely necessary.

RESOURCES FOR FURTHER READING

Atwell, N. (1998). *In the middle: New understandings about writing, reading, and learning* (2nd ed.). Portsmouth, NH: Boynton-Cook.

This second edition will help teachers effectively convey expectations for reading time to their students so that guided reading can be successful. The author explains how to help students "get inside" their roles and responsibilities as readers, and how to reinforce these roles and responsibilities consistently through the fall of a school year. She lists expectations for reading that she shares with her students as well as rules for a reading workshop.

Boushey, G., & Moser, J. (2006). *The daily 5: Fostering literacy independence in the elementary grades.* York, ME: Stenhouse.

The "daily five" is a student-driven management structure designed to fully engage students in reading and writing. The authors show educators how guided reading is possible in a classroom where students are taught how to engage meaningfully and independently in five literacy tasks: reading to self, reading with someone, writing, word work, and listening to reading. A concrete plan for the first 5 weeks of school is provided.

Diller, D. (2003). *Literacy work stations: Making centers work.* York, ME: Stenhouse.

This book, geared toward K–2, offers the suggestion of literacy work stations for the rest of the class during guided reading. The author fully explains how to organize and utilize each suggested work station, and provides photographs as well as reproducibles in English and in Spanish. The author anticipates possible problems for each station and offers troubleshooting ideas. She also offers concrete strategies to ensure that students gain the understanding of work stations needed to be independent learners.

Diller, D. (2005). *Practice with purpose: Literacy work stations for grades 3-6.* York, ME: Stenhouse.

In this book, the author persuades teachers in grades 3–6 that literacy work stations *can* provide meaningful independent learning for students while teachers instruct small groups. After explaining the difference between a literacy work station and a traditional center, she clearly describes how to set up, introduce, and manage each type of literacy work station. The appendices also contain useful resources for each station, such as signs, question cards, and graphic organizers.

Chapter 7

Meaningful Activities for the Rest of the Class

"I spend too much time planning my literacy centers. I feel like I spend more time cutting and pasting, copying and organizing, than my students spend actually working in the centers."

For guided reading to be successful in a classroom, the teacher has to be able to work with each group for 15–20 *uninterrupted* minutes. If a teacher plans to do two groups per day, that means students need to learn to work independently for 30–40 minutes. Responsive guided reading groups work best when they're short and concentrated, and that means the students in that group need their teacher's undivided attention. Traditionally, teachers have been told to use centers during guided reading to occupy the rest of their students. While a center configuration is a fine way to occupy students, center organization can take up a lot of teacher time: in planning differentiated work for each center, assembling materials, training students to use the centers independently, and evaluating the work students do at each center.

As we said in Chapter 6, rather than thinking of centers as the only means for productively occupying students during guided reading, we like to think of this time as "independent literacy activity" time. Small groups of students need not move from one spot in the classroom to another; as long as our students are engaged in independent literacy activities, this can be productive time. We also are aware that some teachers don't have the luxury of having enough space to set up centers in discrete areas of the room. For classes of many students and/or small classroom spaces, sometimes centers are just not practical.

INDEPENDENT LITERACY ACTIVITIES

We have several general principles for independent literacy activities in the classroom that we hope will guide you as you consider what to do with the rest of your class during responsive guided reading.

Principle 1: Keep It Simple

We have witnessed teachers who go overboard in planning independent literacy activities or centers. They put in inordinate amounts of time cutting and pasting, finding appropriate materials, and bending over backwards to make an activity appealing or fun for kids. While this is all valiant, so often it is not necessary and doesn't prompt student learning any more than a simpler version. Teacher effort in putting together independent literacy activities should be minimal and should achieve maximum student learning.

Principle 2: Consistency Is Good

We do not believe that literacy activities need to change each week, each month, or at all. Students appreciate consistency in the classroom. They like to know what to expect of their time. We very much admire Boushey and Moser's *The Daily 5* (2006), which essentially proposes that students be engaged in the same five independent literacy activities throughout the school year: read to self, read to a partner, listen to a book being read, write, and work with words. When students know what to expect each day, they get into a rhythm that allows them to concentrate on the activity itself, and not on constantly learning the procedures and expectations for a new activity. This makes for productive independent work and helps to avoid the need for a lot of teacher oversight.

Principle 3: Independent Activities Should Help to Increase the *Literacy* Achievement of Our Students

While occupying our students so that we can work with responsive guided reading groups is an important goal of our independent literacy activity time, productivity is also important. This time can and should be quite productive in building the independent literacy skills of our students. Keeping this in mind, it is important that whatever activities we choose are literacy-related. This is not the time to finish up a science activity or play a math game. This is the time for students to practice, independently, some of the skills and strategies they've been learning during shared reading, guided reading, writing workshop, or other areas of language arts. As discussed in Chapter 2, we need to remember the importance of balanced literacy instruction, which emphasizes shared, guided, and independent learning. Independent literacy activity time isn't just busy work; it is a time when students are learning how to read and write independently, are practicing literacy skills introduced at other times, and are engaged with and in charge of their own learning.

Principle 4: Independent Literacy Activities Should Be *Differentiated*

As our students are at many different levels, we need to account for different levels of independent skills. Activities can be adapted so that they work for our most skilled as well as our most struggling readers. It isn't enough if the "word work center" has activities that work brilliantly for some students but are either too easy or too difficult for others. For example, if a second-grade classroom has a word-building activity where students are given cards with base words and cards with the endings -*ed* and -*ing*, some students will benefit greatly from this activity. These students will put a base word together with an ending card and then write down the resulting word on a sheet of paper. They must decide when to double the consonant, drop the *e,* or do nothing to the base word when adding the ending. This activity will work well for the students at an average to slightly above average second-grade reading level. However, students who are very strong readers likely will complete the activity in no time at all and be left wondering what to do next. They won't be appropriately challenged, and therefore will get very little out of the activity. Similarly, some of the below-average readers in the class may have difficulty even reading the base words, much less understanding what to do to the word when adding an ending.

That same center can work well for all students. The struggling readers could have a stack of more decodable base words and be responsible for adding only the *s* ending in the center. The advanced readers could have had a stack of prefixes and suffixes to add to the words for an additional challenge.

What kinds of independent literacy activities accomplish the four principles listed above? We have already mentioned the work of Boushey and Moser (2006), and we do indeed recommend that teachers read their book to get a sense of what can be accomplished during independent literacy time. We also recommend the work of Debbie Diller (2003, 2005), whose work on literacy stations has been very influential for us and the teachers with whom we work. Looking at some of the ideas espoused by those authors, we next review how specific independent literacy activities are in line with the four principles. Please note that these activities can work like centers in that students can rotate from one activity to the next (though without necessarily moving from one place to another in the classroom) or teachers may choose to have their entire class work on one activity at a time.

INDEPENDENT READING

A great place to get started with independent literacy activities is independent reading. We all want our students to learn to enjoy reading on their own—to become lifelong readers. Using independent reading as a starting place for occupying the rest of the class during guided reading serves two purposes: (1) It provides an opportunity for students to become comfortable reading on their own; and (2) it requires very little preparation work on the part of the teacher. Independent reading also beautifully accomplishes our four principles for independent literacy activities. Please note that there are variations on independent reading, namely, buddy reading and listening to reading, that are similar in terms of how they meet the principles of independent activities.

Keep It Simple

A well-stocked classroom library is already the goal of many classroom teachers. Once your library is established, utilizing it during independent literacy activities is a very simple task. Certainly, teachers do need to establish ground rules for independent reading time (as discussed in Chapter 6) and help their students learn how to pick engaging books at their independent reading level, but once these things have been well taught during the first month of school, there is very little work required by the teacher to keep this activity going. Materials may change periodically, as you may bring in library books on a particular theme or you may highlight specific books at specific times, but otherwise there is little preparation needed for independent reading activities. Some teachers do ask their students to keep track of books read or to write one- to two-sentence summaries or reviews of their books, but even this activity, once explained and modeled, requires very little extra work on the part of the teacher.

Consistency Is Good

Children respond well to familiarity. Many teachers create a library area that is comfortable, with pillows, reading lamps, and a soft carpet. Knowing ahead of time that they are going to have the opportunity to visit the classroom library and settle in with a good book is an important way for children to develop a comfort and familiarity with independent reading. Though this comfortable environment is certainly nice, teachers who don't have much space shouldn't feel that students won't enjoy reading. It is this consistent exposure to great books that helps lay the groundwork for lifelong reading enjoyment.

Activities Should Be Literacy-Related

When we consider the overall goals of our literacy instruction, we have to keep in mind that one of the most important goals is creating independent readers. As teachers, we teach and model the use of strategies and skills during whole-class shared reading, we provide support to our young readers as they learn to use those strategies and skills during guided reading, but ultimately, we are doing all of that in order to create readers who can pick up a book on their own, and using the skills and strategies they learned in school, make sense of what they read. Therefore, requiring our students to read independently in the classroom is essential. It gives them time to practice.

Activities Should Be Differentiated

The beauty of independent reading time is that it is inherently differentiated. We provide books to students at a variety of levels, and we help our students to find books that they can read, with little difficulty, on their own. As long as we ensure that we have books that reflect the different reading abilities and interests of the students in our classes, independent reading appropriately challenges all of our students.

INDEPENDENT WRITING

Independent writing activities can take many different forms in a classroom. Some teachers ask kids to compose journal entries during this time. Others may use this time for students to continue working on something they started during writing workshop. Still others may provide writing prompts for students to create original pieces that can be done entirely during center time. Whatever form this activity takes, it can readily fit into the guidelines we have laid out for independent literacy activities.

Keep It Simple

Independent writing activities need not be overly complicated. Students likely will need some time to practice "building stamina" for independent writing, as Atwell (1998) suggests we do for independent reading. But once teachers have gotten students comfortably writing for 15 minutes, they will be ready to go. The teacher need only show students what materials to use and whether he or she would like them to write on specific topics.

Consistency Is Good

While writing topics or activities may change, the consistent piece is the writing itself. Students will know from their work during the first month of school that they will need to write for the entire 15 minutes, so that if they finish up their response to one prompt, for example, they will need to start another.

Activities Should Be Literacy-Related

Just as students need practice reading independently in order to become independent readers, so too do students need practice writing independently to become independent writers. Setting aside time, apart from writing workshop, for students to write allows them to begin to think of themselves as writers. In that sense, independent reading and writing are absolutely critical literacy activities to help students begin to see themselves as literate beings.

Activities Should Be Differentiated

Just as with independent reading, independent writing activities are naturally differentiated. Students with different skills write at their own independent level, such that students' responses to the prompt "write about a time when you felt proud of yourself" will clearly be different depending on who is writing it.

WORKING WITH WORDS

Independent literacy activities that focus on phonics, word parts, or vocabulary are often called "word work." This kind of word study lends itself very well to independent work because students need to practice what they are learning in class, and often our students are at very different places in their capabilities. Word work activities sometimes require a bit more setup than the previous two activities, particularly with regards to differentiation, yet it is an essential piece of the independent literacy work we ask students to do in our classes.

Keep It Simple

Thanks to ideas such as "making words" (Cunningham, Hall, & Heggie, 2001), there are many simple yet effective activities to include in a word work center. Making words, which provides the scrambled letters of a specific word, asks students to write down as many two-letter, three-letter, four-letter, and so on, words that they can make using the letters they are given. Sometimes they are given specific hints such as "Make the three-letter word for an animal that barks," and sometimes it is more open-ended. Ultimately, students try to use all of the letters provided to unscramble the original word. Typically a teacher would model how to do this with the whole class, but once students are comfortable with the format, they can do it on their own. Teachers need only change the word/letters on a regular basis, something that takes very little time to do. Similarly, word-building activities (such as the activity with endings mentioned above) require an initial explanation, but otherwise the teacher need only change the word parts included to create a whole new activity.

Consistency Is Good

Just as with independent writing, word work activities will be very stable over the course of the year. Teachers will initially explain the types of materials used for these activities (e.g., letter tiles, word cards, dictionaries, and word game boards) and where to find them, and then they will remain the same throughout the year. We find that having three or four options for word work helps maintain consistency. Teachers offer enough choices to spark student interest over the year, but not so many that it becomes overwhelming or confusing. Table 7.1 lists ideas for word work for younger and older students.

Activities Should Be Literacy-Related

Clearly, any activity that promotes students' understanding of words, either from a phonological- or a vocabulary-related perspective, is literacy-related. Word work activities allow students to practice the skills they learn in class independently. This work will lead to improved word recognition or word understanding when students encounter unknown words while they are reading.

Activities Should Be Differentiated

Students who already have phonemic awareness should not be doing phonemic awareness activities during their independent literacy activity time. By the same token, students who have only recently become comfortable including beginning and ending consonant sounds in their writing shouldn't be working on vowel patterns. What that means is that during word work, teachers will need to know their students and their capabilities. It is not difficult to differentiate word work, but it

TABLE 7.1. Word Work Activities for Different Grade Levels

Grades K–1	Grades 2–5
• Word sorts with phonics patterns	• Vocabulary-related word sorts
• Making words	• Making big words
• Forming letters with clay or in sand	• Word building with base words and affixes
• Handwriting activities	• Word games like Scrabble or Boggle
• Work with classmates' names (e.g., matching with pictures, clapping out syllables, alphabetizing)	• Cursive practice
	• Dictionary practice

does mean that teachers will need to provide different options when students are doing word work. Some word work is easy to differentiate (as in the building words example above). When students are engaging in "making words" activities, they can make words according to their capabilities. Some students may only be able to spell and write two- to three-letter words, while others will be capable of much more. Also, teachers can include "challenge" words that have more letters and that would be suitable for more advanced students. Similarly, teachers can provide word sorts that meet the needs of all students, such that some students may sort words according to the beginning consonant, while others may sort words according to short-*a* word families, while still others may be able to sort words according to all the different sounds that *a* makes.

EXAMPLES OF INDEPENDENT LITERACY ACTIVITIES IN CLASSROOMS

The following figures show how teachers of first and third grades can plan for independent literacy activities, using the ideas contained herein. It also shows how teachers can bring a topic or theme into their centers with very little planning. We only show the first 3 days of the week to demonstrate that within 3 days each group has met with the teacher for guided reading *and* worked through each of the independent literacy activities. On Thursday, you would simply start over with Monday's schedule.

Figure 7.1 shows the plan for a first-grade class that is currently learning about insects in science. You can see that the teacher has incorporated bugs into her independent literacy activities. For independent reading, she has accumulated a binful of books about bugs from her own collection and from the library. She has organized the books according to readability so that students can easily find the "bug book" that is most appropriate for their reading ability. For independent writing, she has provided several prompts, including the following: "Pretend that you are an entomologist. You have discovered a new insect. What does it look like? What does it do? Where does it live? What does it eat? Use markers or crayons to draw your insect and then write a description of it." For word work, she has a making words activity. Each of the words used for making words are the names of insects: *butterfly, beetle, hornet.* In the listening center, she has books by Eric Carle, such as *The Very Hungry Caterpillar* and *The Very Quiet Cricket*, on tape. For her buddy

MONDAY	Group 1	Group 2	Group 3	Group 4	Group 5	Group 6
Session 1	Guided reading	Independent reading: bug books available	Independent writing with insect-related prompts	Buddy reading: nonfiction insect books	Listening center: Eric Carle books	Word work: making words with insect words
Session 2	Word work: making words with insect words	Guided reading	Independent reading: bug books available	Independent writing with insect-related prompts	Buddy reading: nonfiction insect books	Listening center: Eric Carle books
TUESDAY	Group 1	Group 2	Group 3	Group 4	Group 5	Group 6
Session 1	Listening center: Eric Carle books	Word work: making words with insect words	Guided reading	Independent reading: bug books available	Independent writing with insect-related prompts	Buddy reading: nonfiction insect books
Session 2	Buddy reading: nonfiction insect books	Listening center: Eric Carle books	Word work: making words with insect words	Guided reading	Independent reading: bug books available	Independent writing with insect-related prompts
WEDNESDAY	Group 1	Group 2	Group 3	Group 4	Group 5	Group 6
Session 1	Independent writing with insect-related prompts	Buddy reading: nonfiction insect books	Listening center: Eric Carle books	Word work: making words with insect words	Guided reading	Independent reading: bug books available
Session 2	Independent reading: bug books available	Independent writing with insect-related prompts	Buddy reading: nonfiction insect books	Listening center: Eric Carle books	Word work: making words with insect words	Guided reading

FIGURE 7.1. First-grade schedule for guided reading and independent literacy activities.

readers, she has provided some nonfiction books about insects as well as some questions about insects for the buddies to answer.

Note that it is possible, *but not essential*, that independent literacy activities reflect themes or topics of study. A teacher might also have students read any book they select, write on a self-selected topic, make words without a theme involved, and listen to an unrelated book on tape. Many teachers find that varying this practice, that is, sometimes linking independent literacy activities together and sometimes not, is a fresh and reasonable approach.

Figure 7.2 shows how a third-grade teacher plans for guided reading and independent literacy activities. This teacher, whose class is studying the American pioneers in social studies, easily and quickly updates her independent activities to reflect a pioneer theme. For independent reading, the teacher puts books about pioneer times from her own collection and from the library into a special bin for students to browse through. She has books that are written at different reading levels so that each student in class can find an appropriately leveled book. For her independent writing activity she has provided prompts for different kinds of letters students can write, taking on different perspectives. For example, one prompt asks students to pretend they are traveling west in a covered wagon and to write a letter about their journey to someone back home. The word work activity is vocabulary-related, and asks students to read through different books about pioneer times, searching for new words and writing down what they think the words mean, based on the context of the sentence or paragraph. Dictionaries are provided in order for students to see if they are correct. Buddy readers are provided with books rich in facts about the pioneer times, such as *A Pioneer Sampler: The Daily Life of a Pioneer Family in 1840* by Barbara Greenwood and *If You Traveled West in a Covered Wagon* by Ellen Levine. They are asked to take turns reading and writing down the five most interesting facts that they discover as they read. Finally, the teacher has accumulated a collection of American tall tales (e.g., John Henry, Paul Bunyan) for students to hear in the listening center.

MANAGEMENT AND ASSESSMENT OF INDEPENDENT LITERACY ACTIVITIES

Teachers have different ways of managing independent activities. There are many effective ways for ensuring that students know where they

MONDAY	Group 1	Group 2	Group 3	Group 4	Group 5	Group 6
Session 1	Guided reading	Independent reading: pioneer-themed books available	Independent writing: letters reflecting pioneer times	Buddy reading: fact-filled pioneer books	Listening center: American tall tales	Word work: searching for pioneer-related vocabulary
Session 2	Word work: searching for pioneer-related vocabulary	Guided reading	Independent reading: pioneer-themed books available	Independent writing: letters reflecting pioneer times	Buddy reading: fact-filled pioneer books	Listening center: American tall tales
TUESDAY	Group 1	Group 2	Group 3	Group 4	Group 5	Group 6
Session 1	Listening center: American tall tales	Word work: searching for pioneer-related vocabulary	Guided reading	Independent reading: pioneer-themed books available	Independent writing: letters reflecting pioneer times	Buddy reading: fact-filled pioneer books
Session 2	Buddy reading: fact-filled pioneer books	Listening center: American tall tales	Word work: searching for pioneer-related vocabulary	Guided reading	Independent reading: pioneer-themed books available	Independent writing: letters reflecting pioneer times
WEDNESDAY	Group 1	Group 2	Group 3	Group 4	Group 5	Group 6
Session 1	Independent writing: letters reflecting pioneer times	Buddy reading: fact-filled pioneer books	Listening center: American tall tales	Word work: searching for pioneer-related vocabulary	Guided reading	Independent reading: pioneer-themed books available
Session 2	Independent reading: pioneer-themed books available	Independent writing: letters reflecting pioneer times	Buddy reading: fact-filled pioneer books	Listening center: American tall tales	Word work: searching for pioneer-related vocabulary	Guided reading

FIGURE 7.2. Third-grade schedule for guided reading and independent literacy activities.

need to be at any given time. We think it is important for students to be self-sufficient in this process. Whatever system a teacher has should be clearly explained to students during the first month of school and practiced with teacher oversight so that students can get the hang of it before teachers expect students to do it on their own. We again favor simplicity. A poster similar to the preceding figures (but with fewer details) can be posted permanently in the classroom. Students need to know what group they are in, what day it is, and whether it's the first or second session of the day. With that information, they can be taught how to find the activity they are scheduled to do. With younger kids, you can use picture cues to help students understand, and you may also want to post only one day's activities at a time. In addition, some teachers use student pictures, glued to clothes pins, to provide a visual cue to group membership (see Figure 7.3).

Some teachers may find that it's easier to manage guided reading and independent literacy activities at once by asking the rest of the class to work on only one activity at a time. For example, while a teacher is working with a guided reading group, he or she may prefer that everyone else be engaged in the same task. This task may change day to day, but with this setup, the teacher doesn't have to worry about who's supposed to be where during guided reading. Figure 7.4 illustrates how a teacher may plan for this approach.

	Group 1	Group 2	Group 3	Group 4	Group 5	Group 6
A	Guided Reading	Read to Self	Writing	Read with Buddy	Listen to Book	Word Work ABCDE FGHIJ KLMNO PQRST UVWXYZ
B	Word Work ABCDE FGHIJ KLMNO PQRST UVWXYZ	Guided Reading	Read to Self	Writing	Read with Buddy	Listen to Book

FIGURE 7.3. Example of kindergarten or first-grade literacy activity poster.

	Group 1	Group 2	Group 3	Group 4	Group 5	Group 6
MONDAY						
Session 1	Guided reading	Independent reading: pioneer-themed books	Independent reading: pioneer-themed books	Independent reading: pioneer-themed books	Independent reading: pioneer-themed books	Independent reading: pioneer-themed books
Session 2	Independent writing: letters reflecting pioneer times	Guided reading	Independent writing: letters reflecting pioneer times	Independent writing: letters reflecting pioneer times	Independent writing: letters reflecting pioneer times	Independent writing: letters reflecting pioneer times
TUESDAY	Group 1	Group 2	Group 3	Group 4	Group 5	Group 6
Session 1	Buddy reading: fact-filled pioneer books	Buddy reading: fact-filled pioneer books	Guided reading	Buddy reading: fact-filled pioneer books	Buddy reading: fact-filled pioneer books	Buddy reading: fact-filled pioneer books
Session 2	Independent reading: pioneer-themed books	Independent reading: pioneer-themed books	Independent reading: pioneer-themed books	Guided reading	Listening center: American tall tales	Listening center: American tall tales
WEDNESDAY	Group 1	Group 2	Group 3	Group 4	Group 5	Group 6
Session 1	Word work: searching for pioneer-related vocabulary	Word work: searching for pioneer-related vocabulary	Word work: searching for pioneer-related vocabulary	Word work: searching for pioneer-related vocabulary	Guided reading	Word work: searching for pioneer-related vocabulary
Session 2	Independent reading: pioneer-themed books	Independent reading: pioneer-themed books	Independent reading: pioneer-themed books	Independent reading: pioneer-themed books	Independent reading: pioneer-themed books	Guided reading

FIGURE 7.4. Third-grade schedule for independent literacy activities (all students do the same).

Regarding assessment, we understand that teachers want to make sure that students make productive use of their independent time, but we do not think that asking teachers to bring piles of work home is very realistic or necessary. Teachers can use small amounts of class time to check in with students about their independent work. For example, we know teachers who take 5–10 minutes each day or several times per week to ask students to talk about (in a whole-class or small-group setting) the following questions:

> "What is one thing you learned during your independent work today?"
> "What challenges did you face?"
> "What went well?"
> "What didn't go so well?"

Other teachers meet with only one guided reading group on Fridays and spend the rest of the time allowing students to share one thing they did during independent literacy work that they are especially proud of or happy about. Sometimes this means they do a book talk about a book they read during independent reading or they read a piece of writing they worked on. Buddy readers can share a fact they both agreed was interesting or choral read a passage they liked. This opportunity to share or reflect provides just enough oversight on the part of the teacher that students realize they are being held accountable for the work they do during their independent work.

Teachers who feel comfortable doing so may want to provide their students with independent literacy folders where students can put their completed work from each activity. Periodically, teachers can check these folders and make sure that student work is meeting their expectations. This also allows teachers to check on individual students about whom they may be having concerns.

RESOURCES FOR FURTHER READING

Boushey, G., & Moser, J. (2006). *The daily 5: Fostering literacy independence in the elementary schools.* York, ME: Stenhouse.

The authors show educators how guided reading is possible in a classroom where students are taught how to engage meaningfully and independently in five literacy tasks: reading to self, reading with someone, writing, word work, and listening to reading. They explicitly teach educators how to implement a plan focused on students taking responsibility for their own learning and behavior. A concrete outline for the first 5 weeks of school is provided.

Diller, D. (2003). *Literacy work stations: Making centers work.* York, ME: Stenhouse.

This book, geared toward K–2, offers the suggestion of literacy work stations for "the rest of the class" during guided reading. The author fully explains how to organize and utilize each suggested work station, and provides photographs as well as reproducibles in English and in Spanish. Some of the work stations suggested are a big book work station, a drama work station, and an ABC/word study work station. The author also anticipates possible problems for each station and offers troubleshooting ideas.

Diller, D. (2005). *Practice with purpose: Literacy work stations for grades 3–6.* York, ME: Stenhouse.

In this book, the author persuades teachers in grades 3–6 that literacy work stations *can* provide meaningful independent learning for students while teachers instruct small groups. After explaining the difference between a literacy work station and a traditional center, Diller clearly describes how to set up and manage each type of literacy work station. The appendices contain useful resources for each station such as signs, question cards, and graphic organizers.

Guastello, E. F., & Lenz, C. R. (2007). *The guided reading kidstation model: Making instruction meaningful for the whole class.* Newark, DE: International Reading Association.

In the kidstation model, students work productively on standards-based activities at *kid stations*. The authors present a plan using four kid stations and a 5-day cycle. Each kid station addresses one of the first four language arts standards. Essential to the model is that students present their completed work accomplished in their kid station groups to their classmates weekly.

Owocki, G. (2005). *Time for literacy centers: How to organize and differentiate instruction.* Portsmouth, NH: Heinemann.

The author explains how to organize and maintain effective learning centers that meet students' different needs. She explains each of her over 50 center ideas by listing needed materials, possible activities, and preparation and instruction. Some center ideas include drama and retelling, alphabet book writing, and language transcription.

Southall, M. (2007). *Differentiated literacy centers: 85+ leveled activities—with reproducible planning sheets and student pages—to support centers in fluency, reading comprehension, and word study.* New York: Scholastic.

The author shares dozens of ready-to-use activities at three levels of challenge that help children work successfully on their own in grades K–3. She also explains a workable framework that makes setting up the centers and tracking student progress simple. Ready-to-go planning sheets and record-keeping forms are provided.

Chapter 8

Assessing Students for Placement in Responsive Guided Reading Groups

*"I am so afraid I won't get it right—
that I'll put my students in groups
that are not right for them at all."*

The great thing about accepting ahead of time the idea that you will devote the entire month of September to preparing your students for responsive guided reading and the rest of the literacy block is that the month gives you time to make both informal observations about your students' reading and to do more explicit assessment of students.

TEACHER OBSERVATIONS

We don't recommend that you start right away with specific reading assessments, such as fluency snapshots or running records. These can feel overwhelming to students as they get back into the routine of being at school and working with a group. It is more important to spend the first couple weeks building classroom community and making sure that students feel comfortable in the classroom environment. These early days are when students learn the rules of your class, forge friendships with their classmates, and come to learn the routine.

But the first weeks of school *are* an ideal time to begin your own informal observations of students. Learning about the literacy experiences and practices of your students will reveal important details about them. Some teachers ask students to bring their favorite book to class and show it to their classmates. Even from this simple activity, you can learn a lot about the literacy practices of your students. What *is* each student's favorite book? Was this activity comparably harder for some of your students, who may not have a lot of books at home? Was this a book that the child's parents read to her? Was it a book the teacher read in class the prior year? Can the child read the book by himself? How does the child act when talking about the book? Does she seem very excited about sharing a book? Thinking about these questions will help you draw some preliminary conclusions about each student's experiences with reading.

Another thing that some teachers do at the beginning of the school year is administer a reading interest survey. These surveys ask students if they like to read, how often they read, what books they've read lately, how many books they have at home, and other details of their literacy experiences. They also ask students to consider what kinds of books they like to read best, and also whether or not they read materials other than books. A teacher can learn so much about a child from a simple one- or two-page survey. It's helpful to know which of your students consider themselves readers and which ones don't; which ones read a lot at home, and which don't; which ones have been read to and which haven't. This information will not help you to understand the reading levels of students, but it will give you insights into their affective response to reading, as well as their motivation. Knowing, too, what kinds of books each student typically would choose to read helps you to consider what kinds of books/materials you should have in your classroom library, and can begin to help you assist students in selecting texts that will be of interest to them.

In this beginning period, while you are not doing responsive guided reading groups or independent literacy activities yet, you will still be doing a lot of reading—shared reading and read-alouds—with the whole class. These whole-group activities will also afford you the opportunity to learn a lot about your students. A kindergarten teacher who reads a big book aloud to her students will learn very quickly which of her students have concepts of print (i.e., the understanding that print goes left to right, up to down, and other basic details about the way print operates) (Clay, 2006) simply by regularly asking questions such as, "Who can point to the front cover of this book?," "Who can point to the words as I read them?," "Who can turn the pages for me as I read?" Similarly, the same teacher can learn about students' alphabetic knowledge or phonological awareness by asking questions like, "Who can see a word that begins with the letter *b*?" or "Which word do you hear that rhymes with *bear*?" By scanning the class during such a lesson, it is not difficult to see which students are waving their hands wildly, eager to participate, and which are much less sure of themselves.

Teachers of older students can also learn a lot during shared reading. A shared reading lesson that focuses on vocabulary, for example, allows a teacher to determine the word knowledge of his or her students. By pulling out of the shared reading certain challenging words, a teacher can quickly assess which of his or her students already know the words or has a strategy available in order to make an educated guess about them, as well as which students don't know the words and don't have any idea how to figure them out.

The read-aloud time in your class will also allow you to learn about your students. As you read aloud, scan the class. Who is following along with your every word? Who is asking questions as you read to try to make meaning of the book? Who is able to answer the questions you pose as you read? Who cannot answer questions or makes seemingly irrelevant comments? Who is checked out? Who is misbehaving? Who is lying down or rolling around? As you begin to answer these questions, you are going to get a very good initial understanding of your students' engagement with reading, their interest in and understanding of the materials you read, and even a sense of their reading strengths and weaknesses. We urge you to take notes about your observations because these notes will be very helpful as you begin to think about how your students will be placed in responsive guided reading groups. A teacher who makes careful observations and is really in tune with his or her students during these early days of school will likely learn a lot more about these students than he or she would ever believe possible.

After observing and thinking about the literacy engagement and abilities of each student in your class during these first weeks, you may begin to consider how your students compare to your expectations for this grade. At first it's helpful to think about it in this way: Which students seem to be exceeding your expectations? Meeting your expectations? Which ones do not seem to be where you'd expect them to be for the grade level you teach? If you can sort them into just these three basic groups in your head, this will give you a baseline against which to weigh the assessment data you collect over the next 2 weeks.

USING READING ASSESSMENTS TO MAKE GROUPING DECISIONS: KINDERGARTEN

We take seriously the words of Ford and Opitz: "Our job as teachers is to determine what the child already knows and what the child needs to learn, then to design instruction accordingly" (2008, p. 74). After you have spent the first couple of weeks of school getting to know your students, bonding with them, helping them to acclimate into your classroom environment, and making informal observations about their learning, it is important to spend some time over the next several weeks doing reading assessments to get a clearer sense of their reading strengths and weaknesses. One of the nice things about devoting the first month of school to learning routines and procedures is that while your students are practicing how to work independently and building their "stamina" for literacy work, you can pull students one at a time to do assessments. For kindergarten-age students, we recommend that you assess students' concepts of print, alphabet letter recognition, phonemic awareness, and phonological awareness. For more advanced kindergartners, you may also want to assess word recognition and spelling. (Please note that all of these areas of emergent literacy are typically included in early literacy assessments such as DIBELS [Dynamic Indicators of Basic Early Literacy Skills] and ELSA (Early Literacy Skills Assessment]). As you're assessing your kindergartners, you should be mentally considering which of your students fall into three specific categories. Examples of these categories are included in Table 8.1.

It will become clear from these assessments if there are some students who are lacking most of the skills that you would expect incoming kindergartners to have. These students will need to work together in a small group in order to more effectively learn those skills. Similarly, those students who know their alphabet letters but do not know the sounds the letters make would work together. See Figure 8.1 for a sense of what your kindergarten groups might look like at the beginning of the school year (before many or most of them are even reading).

Early in the school year, the teacher will be working with small groups, though in kindergarten he or she won't be using leveled readers with all groups except the last. Rather, he or she will be doing word work that will look very different depending on the group. For example, with Group 1, the teacher will be solidifying the concepts of print by doing a lot of work with book handling. Furthermore, he or she will do a lot of work on the letters of the alphabet as well as rhyming and alliteration. With Group 2, the teacher will be doing a lot of work on

TABLE 8.1. Three Initial Categories for Considering Emergent Literacy Skills of Kindergartners

Approaching expectations
- Unclear on concepts of print
- Recognizes fewer than half of the alphabet letters (uppercase)
- Cannot write most alphabet letters
- Difficulty listening to a story
- Lacks basic phonemic awareness, such as ability to hear rhyme or alliteration
- Knows few if any letter sounds

Meeting expectations
- Understands most concepts of print
- Recognizes the majority of alphabet letters
- Writes some of the alphabet letters
- Can follow along and engage with a read-aloud
- Has some phonemic awareness, including ability to hear rhymes and initial consonant sounds
- Knows common consonant letter sounds (*b, d, f, k, l, m, n, p, s, t*)
- Recognizes some high-frequency words (*no, yes, stop, on*)

Exceeding expectations
- Recognizes upper- and lowercase alphabet letters
- Writes all or most alphabet letters
- Highly engaged in read-aloud
- Well-developed phonemic awareness, including onset and rhyme and phonemic segmentation
- Knows most letter sounds, including some vowels
- Recognizes a lot of high-frequency words
- May be able to read

phonemic awareness, and will want to make sure the group is solid with their alphabet letters. Group 3 will work on more advanced phonemic awareness and letter sounds. Group 4 is on the cusp of being able to read, so the teacher may work with high-frequency word recognition as well as word family work. Group 5 will be ready to start with early leveled readers, so they'll be more like a guided reading group. Throughout the year, each of the groups will begin to read books as well, as they master the early literacy skills. By January, most groups will start using books during responsive guided reading, though they may continue to practice their phonemic and phonological skills in many places in the literacy day.

GROUPING IN FIRST GRADE AND BEYOND

First-grade teachers will need to use some of the same assessments as kindergarten teachers, and consider grouping decisions based on the categories provided above. In spite of our best efforts in kindergarten,

Group 1: Students who lack concepts of print and word; don't know any or most alphabet letters; lack basic phonemic awareness (trouble even with rhyming words and alliteration).

Group 2: Students who know most but not all of uppercase alphabet letters but not all lowercase letters; recognize rhyme and alliteration but unable to distinguish onset and rime; know some consonant sounds.

Group 3: Students who know all or most of their alphabet letters (upper- and lowercase); phonemic awareness includes ability to distinguish onset and rime, though not letter-by-letter phonemic segmentation; know some consonant sounds; recognize some words in print.

Group 4: Students who recognize all their alphabet letters; are able to segment individual phonemes in words; know most consonant sounds and some vowel sounds; inventive spelling includes initial and final consonants and some vowels; recognize some high-frequency words.

Group 5: Students who are already able to read some very early readers; know short-vowel sounds; inventive spelling includes initial and final consonants with accurate use of short vowels.

FIGURE 8.1. Sample characteristics of kindergarten groups.

there are certainly some students who will enter first grade unable to read, and with varying degrees of phonological skills. For those students who enter first grade reading (and for students in second to fifth grades), it is important to get a sense of how well they read, and what level of material they are capable of reading. Thus, they will participate in the kinds of assessments appropriate for older kids.

Assessing students' reading at the beginning of the school year is an ability that comes over time. Therefore, while we believe that a running record (Clay, 2000) is the best way to pinpoint students' reading strengths and weaknesses as well as an exact reading level (we discuss their use below), we also acknowledge how difficult that can be for teachers new to the profession or new to that particular assessment. We firmly believe that the most important thing is to get students placed into groups as soon as possible (but after the training month). Therefore, we advise grade 2–5 teachers to begin with fluency snapshots (Blachowicz & Ogle, 2001).

Fluency Snapshots

Fluency snapshots (or curriculum-based measurements, also referred to as CBMs) are 1-minute assessments that are easy to administer and easy to score. A student reads aloud from a passage for 1 minute, the teacher circles all errors (substitutions, mispronunciations, omissions, and words students don't even attempt) and then determines how many words the student has read accurately in 1 minute. The resulting words correct per minute (WCPM) can be compared to grade-level norms provided with most assessments so that teachers can easily see how their students measure up compared to the norming sample for that grade. While fluency snapshots are limited in the kind of information they provide, they do give us a "rough cut" for drawing conclusions about our students' reading strengths and weaknesses. Most teachers who use fluency snapshots fully acknowledge that they do not measure comprehension specifically, and that this omission may skew the data. However, fluency snapshots have been shown to correlate to more extensive (and time-consuming) assessments that do measure comprehension acuity, and thus are useful for an overview of the class reading ability. They certainly don't tell the whole story, but they may tell enough to begin to group students knowing full well that movement between groups is an expected part of classroom practices.

There are several ways to use the results of a fluency snapshot as information to place students in responsive guided reading groups. First, we can determine which of our students are at, above, and below grade level. We do so by comparing their WCPM with their grade-level norms. We will have the ability, then, to sort students by above, at, and below grade-level fluency levels. Once we've divided our class into these three groups, we can look further into the fluency snapshot and use other observation data to group kids into still smaller groups. For more information on administering and analyzing fluency snapshots, please refer to Blachowicz, Sullivan, and Cieply (2001). Figure 8.2 shows how a third-grade teacher might group his or her students based on the fluency snapshot.

Using Running Records to Fine-Tune Responsive Guided Reading Groups

If time allows during your first month of school, it can be quite helpful to do running records with at least some students in order to get a sense of appropriate instructional level. Running records (Clay, 2000) provide much more information about our students' reading level than do fluency snapshots. We determine with much more precision a student's reading level and can also begin to understand some of his or her strengths and weaknesses. We also analyze miscues in order to determine the kinds of errors a student is making while he or she reads

Group 1: Students reading fewer than 30 WCPM, placing them at or near the 10th percentile of the third-grade norms. The fluency snapshot passage was clearly too difficult for them, as they even stumbled over some third-grade sight words. (two students)

Group 2: Students reading between 30 and 50 WCPM, placing them between the 15th and 30th percentile of the third-grade norms. Though the students struggled with decoding, it wasn't nearly as much of a struggle as for the students in Group 1. (three students)

Group 3: Students reading between 60 and 80 WCPM, placing them at or near the 50th percentile. These students did not struggle much at all with decoding, except for multisyllabic and lower-frequency words. (six students)

Group 4: Students reading between 80 and 100 WCPM, placing them at or just below the 75th percentile for third-grade norms. Students had no trouble with decoding, miscued infrequently, and seemed very confident in their reading. (seven students)

Group 5: Students reading above 100 WCPM, placing them in the top quartile of the third-grade norms. Students read even multisyllabic words accurately, and had no more than two miscues. (six students)

FIGURE 8.2. Sample third-grade groups based on fluency snapshot.

and which cueing systems (graphophonic, syntactic, and semantic) are being used and how well. After giving a running record, we can say with much more confidence and evidence exactly what level a student is reading at and what his or her strengths and weaknesses are in reading.

While we do believe it is ideal to administer running records to all students in a class, we acknowledge how much time that can take, and how difficult it can be to find that time at the beginning of the school year, particularly for novice teachers. For these reasons, we suggest that you start with those students that are either clearly below or clearly above level. Looking at Figure 8.2 again, it would probably be very helpful to do running records with the students in Groups 1 and 2, as these students are below level, but from a fluency snapshot we cannot determine how far below grade level they are. A running record would provide that information. Similarly, a running record would help us with Group 5, as we determine how far above grade level the students are.

If time permits, it would be wonderful to be able to do a running record with each student, to determine if your conclusions from the fluency snapshots are accurate and to get a better sense of which students belong together in a responsive guided reading group.

JUST GET STARTED

We do not want the above section to intimidate the novice teacher. Running records are a very helpful assessment, but it is possible to get started with responsive guided reading without doing them. In fact, we believe it is beneficial just to get started with responsive guided reading even before we're sure we've got the groups just right. One important thing to remember about responsive guided reading is that groups can and should change. So, if you have used the results of the fluency snapshot as well as your own impressions and observations of the students in your class to create groups, it is perfectly acceptable and desirable to just get started. If you find after a day or two that you have put a student into the higher group who is now struggling with reading the materials the group is reading, it is okay to move that student. If you have placed a child in the lower group and it becomes very clear that while his rate of reading is slow, his decoding is strong, as is his comprehension, it is okay to move him. Teachers can even explain this up front, letting students know that you've placed them in groups and that you want to get started with reading with the groups right away, but that membership in a group could change at any time as you become more familiar with the skills and strategies that your students possess. (For much more on the flexibility of responsive guided reading groups, see Chapter 9.) Once you get started, you'll see whether or not you've placed students well, and you'll be able to make changes as necessary.

We feel strongly that teachers' observations should not be discounted, even when assessment data doesn't confirm their initial impressions. For example, a second-grade teacher may notice that a child is very engaged in read-alouds, participating frequently and freely. The same child may have a tremendous vocabulary during class discussions about the read-aloud and may generally seem to love reading. Initially, this student may seem to meet expectations or even exceed them for the beginning of second grade. However, when the teacher goes on to do a fluency snapshot with a second-grade passage, he or she may find that the same student is reading slowly and spending too much time decoding words that the child should be reading automatically at this grade. What does a teacher do with this seemingly contradictory information? Does this mean that the teacher's initial impressions of the student were wrong? Too often, teachers jettison their own conclusions and insights when faced with assessment data that doesn't fit. Teachers need to keep all of the information they collect, including their own observations, in mind when grouping students. It is possible that this child was nervous during the fluency snapshot, or the passage read may have been on a topic with which the student had no prior experience. A good teacher will keep a close eye on this student and be willing to move her into another group if the placement turns out to be incorrect.

RESOURCES FOR FURTHER READING

Barr, R., Blachowicz, C., Bates, A., Katz, C., & Kaufman, B. (2006). *Reading diagnosis for teachers: An instructional approach* (5th ed.). Boston: Allyn & Bacon.

This book is a "must" for educators who want strategies to assess students informally in each area of reading. Chapters on knowledge of print, oral reading, vocabulary, and reading comprehension explain multiple ways to assess and give instructional support in each area. Helpful appendices include an example of an informal reading inventory (IRI), a list of assessment instruments, and resources for leveling books.

Clay, M. M. (2000). *Running records: For classroom teachers.* Portsmouth, NH: Heinemann.

The author introduces key ideas about using running records to drive instruction. She explains why to use them, how they relate to teaching, and how to administer them. Two options for scoring are provided. One focuses solely on accuracy; the other focuses on analyzing how the reader problemsolves while working on a text.

Clay, M. M. (2007). *An observation survey of early literacy achievement.* Portsmouth, NH: Heinemann.

The author presents systematic observation measurement tasks that help teachers to observe a young child's oral language, concepts about print, the reading of continuous text, letter knowledge, reading and writing vocabulary, phonemic awareness, and phonics. She explains how carefully recorded observation can guide instruction, and she provides suggestions in each of the aforementioned areas.

McKenna, M. C., & Dougherty Stahl, K. A. (2009). *Assessment for reading instruction* (2nd ed.). New York: Guilford Press.

This book is filled with effective ways to evaluate the spelling, word recognition, fluency, comprehension, and strategic knowledge of students, in grades K–6. Some assessments are described and recommended while others are available within the book. The authors also discuss how to use the results to strategically inform instruction.

Robb, L. (2009). *Assessments for differentiating reading instruction: 100 forms and checklists for identifying students' strengths so you can help every reader improve.* New York: Scholastic.

This book will help teachers use performance-based assessments to make instructional decisions that will foster students' reading, writing, thinking, and speaking. It includes over 100 reproducibles on an accompanying CD. Some of the focuses are comprehension, conferences, and self-evaluation.

Wilde, S. (2000). *Miscue analysis made easy: Building on students' strengths*. Portsmouth, NH: Heinemann.

The author makes a case for employing miscue analysis to identify students' reading strengths and using this information to support their further learning. The book offers information to help educators understand the reading process as well as the practice of using miscue analysis. The author offers ideas for how to use miscue analysis as well as simplified versions of it within a progressive reading model.

Chapter 9

Moving Students in and out of Groups

*"I know my students aren't supposed to stay
in the same group all year, but the idea
of moving them around according to their
learning needs is too complicated.
Honestly, I rarely change my groups."*

One of the ways that current guided reading practices are different, theoretically, from reading groups in the past is that groups are flexible and changing throughout the school year. At one time, reading groups were nearly the same as tracking. Students were assessed at the beginning of the school year and placed in groups that never changed during the year, and changed very little from year to year. In other words, if you were in the "low group" in first grade, you were often still in the low group in fifth grade. We know now that this is an inappropriate way to approach guided reading. One of the features of guided reading, according to Fountas and Pinnell (1996), one that we endorse, is that grouping is *not* tracking, and should instead reflect individual student capabilities at particular moments in time. Teachers should not limit their assessment to the beginning of the school year, but rather should assess, formally and informally, their students throughout the school year in order to determine appropriate group placement. The goal of guided reading is to help students become better readers. If the readers in our low group do not ever shift out of that low group, then we need to consider whether or not guided reading is serving a purpose in our classrooms. We also remind teachers that every time you listen to students reading you are assessing them. Assessment is not defined by instrumentation or recording mechanisms, but rather by information gathering—and much information is gathered as teachers listen to students read in the responsive guided reading group.

That being said, however, there is much in the literature that refers to grouping that is more heterogeneous in nature, that addresses particular student *needs* regardless of ability. For example, a teacher could notice that he or she has several students who have a hard time using visualization as a technique for comprehension. He or she could, conceivably, pull these students together for a guided reading group, even though they are at three different reading levels, in order to provide extra practice on visualization. This kind of grouping is certainly useful, but it not only requires extreme flexibility on the part of the teacher but also an ability to regularly pinpoint the specific strengths and weaknesses of each student. Not surprisingly, this is where many teachers have difficulties. We advocate for frequent assessment of students in order to make sure they are receiving the instruction they need, but we also know, from our interactions with teachers, that the ability to form and reform groups based on specific needs can be difficult in practice. Responsive guided groups can and should be flexible, but the groups do not need to shift so regularly that students and teachers alike are left with their heads spinning.

WHAT DOES FLEXIBLE GROUPING LOOK LIKE IN RESPONSIVE GUIDED READING?

As we stated in Chapter 8, our goal when initially placing kids in responsive guided reading groups is to do so based on good assessment data and our own informal observations of our students. However, we also need to get our students in groups as quickly as possible. We know teachers who are loathe to get started with guided reading groups until they are *absolutely sure* they have placed students in *exactly* the right group. We believe that responsive guided reading groups need to get started as soon as possible (ideally by October), and therefore, if we mistakenly place a child in a higher group than turns out to be appropriate, that is okay. With flexible groups, we can easily remedy that problem by reassigning that child to a different group. Students need to know that the groups they are in are not set in stone and that they may move around often. They also need to know that being moved into one group and out of another does not mean that the student is doing anything necessarily wrong or necessarily right. Movement is neither punitive nor a cause for celebration. Teachers can and should be very clear about responsive guided reading groups: how they are intended to help children become even stronger readers, and how students may be switched around during the year for a variety of reasons.

There are two ways that we propose teachers reevaluate and regroup students: the first is at two preestablished points during the school year; the second is on an as-needed basis. We explore these two options in the following two sections.

REVISITING GROUPING DECISIONS
TWICE PER YEAR

We strongly recommend that responsive guided reading grouping decisions be "officially" revisited at least twice per year, in January and again in March. This is best done using running records, or possibly a combination of running records (for more information on administering and analyzing running records, please refer to Fountas and Pinnell, 1996, or Clay, 2000) and fluency snapshots. Note that while administering fluency snapshots at the beginning of the year is a good way to get a "rough cut" of how students are reading, we don't recommend them as the sole means of reassessing students in January or March. They simply do not provide enough information. You can tell roughly who is reading above, at, and below grade level, but we believe there are finer gradations than those three levels that are important to learn after students have been in responsive guided reading groups for several months in order to make meaningful changes in groups. Teacher judgment and observations will also play a key role at these two times, as they do throughout the year.

Just as teachers can use running records to get a better understanding of students' reading strengths and weaknesses at the beginning of the school year than a fluency snapshot provides, so too they can use running records at several time points throughout the year to renew their understanding of students' reading strengths and weaknesses. They can also be used to reassess students' instructional reading levels. Even if a teacher is not able to do running records in September, we do recommend that teachers make every effort to administer running records in January, after students return from winter break. This provides the teacher with two points of information: First of all, it can help you to see how each student has developed over the first portion of the school year. For example, a second-grade teacher may have devoted a lot of her shared reading time during the fall to decoding multisyllabic words and using graphophonic cues in the middle and at the end of words. She may discover from administering running records in January that many of her students are decoding multisyllabic words with much more facility and that she can deemphasize that skill during her instruction. Similarly, she may discover that some students' miscues reflect inattention to meaning and that she may need to focus her instruction on self-monitoring while reading. While responsive guided reading addresses student needs whatever they may be, it is helpful for the teacher to get a sense of what areas are most in need of addressing during shared reading.

Another thing that running records can tell teachers is the precise instructional level of their students (e.g., the reading level at which students can read 90–95% of the text accurately). This information should be used to consider whether or not students are still appropriately placed within their responsive guided reading groups. A teacher can explain to his or her class, "Just like we switch our seating clusters around from time to time, we're also going to switch our reading groups from time to time." If teachers explain this up front, students are less likely to think they're not measuring up in reading.

A teacher may find, after reassessing his or her students in January (or March) that there are too many students reading at a given level to make one reading group feasible. We know from our conversations with teachers that some teachers will not move students because they are worried about their groups being too big. We strongly recommend that if this does happen within your classroom that you split the group in two. For example, if you already have a large group of seven students in your top reading group and you realize after reassessing students that you have two more students reading at the same level, it makes more sense to create two "top" groups of four and five than to force those two children to read at a level that is too easy for them. Children who are given materials that are not challenging enough during responsive guided reading tend to breeze through their readings quickly (causing potential behavior challenges), and they will not likely miscue enough to make the one-on-one time with the teacher productive.

If it feels like the number of groups in your classroom has become unmanageable, you may want to take an inventory of your currently existing groups to see if you can make changes. For example, in our conversations with classroom teachers, we have found that the most struggling readers are often in a "group" by themselves because these readers are often so far behind the rest of the class that it wouldn't be appropriate to put them in a group with other students. Another option for that struggling reader is to consider placing him or her with the students that are at the next level up. Because responsive guided reading doesn't focus on brand-new instruction, but rather on practicing strategies already learned while teachers listen to students read, there is no reason that you could not work with a group of readers that are at slightly different levels, reading different materials.

Consider the following example from a first-grade classroom.

Mrs. Bevington, a first-grade teacher, has five reading groups in her class. In the fall, her top reading group has seven students, and she meets with them once or twice per week. Her next two groups have six students each, and she meets with each twice a week. Her next group has four students, whom she meets with twice a week, and her final group has two students, whom she tries to see three times a week. This arrangement works just fine for Mrs. Bevington. She is comfortable working with five groups, and she feels like she is able to provide good instruction to each of her students. However, in January when she reevaluates her groups, she realizes that there has been a lot of growth for many of her students. When she examines the results of the running records, she realizes that she now has 10 students who could be reading together in her top group, and that several others have also moved up in reading levels, including one of the students in her lowest reading group. She realizes, too, that a couple of her students may have been working with materials that were too challenging for them. When she attempts to create new groups, considering students' instructional levels, she comes up with the following arrangement: 10 students in her top group, six students each in the next two groups, two students in the next group, and one student in her last group. She does not think that a group of 10 students is workable and she is tempted to keep a few of the students in a lower group. After consulting with the literacy coach at her school, she decides she will try something new for her. She will split the top group into two groups of five students each. She also decides to combine her lowest reader with the two students in the next group up. She is relieved to have smaller groups now, as even seven students seemed slightly unwieldy to her. The first time she calls her group of three, she explains to them that they will be working together in a group, even though they won't always be reading the same book. For their first meeting, she has found a book about sharks that is at the reading level of two of the students and a book about underwater life for her lowest reader. She quickly reviews nonfiction texts, reminding students that the information they read is true, that they should look at the photographs in the two books, and she asks the students to consider what questions they may have about sharks and/or life in the ocean. Then they start reading. Although the students are reading different texts, she is still able to listen to each read and provide support as necessary. When she has listened to each student read, they are able to have a postreading wrap-up, with each student sharing something he or she has learned during the reading. Mrs. Bevington is satisfied with this arrangement. She feels that she can find books that are similar in content and still reinforce reading strategies and provide individualized support.

While we do believe it would be ideal if students would fall neatly into five equal groups of five or six, we know that in reality it doesn't always (or even often) work that way. We encourage teachers to be creative with their groupings to ensure that students can work in groups and with materials that challenge them appropriately. We like the arrangement that Mrs. Bevington, above, has created. Rather than hold students back for fear of having a reading group that was too big, she split the group in two, resulting in two groups of five instead of a group of 10. Rather than isolating her lowest reader in a group by herself, she pulled her into the next group up, and came up with a creative solution for including her while also using appropriate materials. She will need to reevaluate these groups, of course, to make sure that students are getting the most out of their responsive guided reading experiences, but this is a reasonable solution for now.

Another reason we like Mrs. Bevington's approach is that, while we may tell ourselves that kids don't really notice groupings, and that we don't make a big deal about who is in which group, it is very obvious to all the students in the class when one child is in a group by him- or herself. Kids draw conclusions based on their observations about group membership that can be unfair or insulting (such as "Jenny's not a good reader" or "Jenny is slow") simply because they see that Jenny is the only student reading alone with the teacher during guided reading. Also, there is something to be said for being part of a group—the "we're all in this together" mentality. When students work together, they form a team, and during guided reading that team membership can be an important motivator for working hard and learning as much as possible. Routman (2002) expands further on this point:

> For guided reading ... the social aspects of learning are also paramount: that is, in a congenial environment of acceptance and trust, students are encouraged to share their thinking, try out what they've been learning, and, with teacher support, approximate, regulate, and expand their reading competency. (p. 152)

REVISITING GROUPING DECISIONS
ON AN AS-NEEDED BASIS

While we advocate officially revisiting groupings for responsive guided reading twice per year, changes may need to be made in between those official time points. In Chapter 8, we advocate getting students into groups by mid-October at the latest (except in kindergarten, where it may take a bit longer), with the knowledge that our groups may not be perfect. We will likely know very quickly if we have misplaced a student, either because we notice that the child is not miscuing at all with the materials we're using, or because the materials we're using are clearly at the child's frustration level. In that situation, we don't need to wait until January to make a change: the change can be made immediately.

Classroom teachers need to be very clear about the fact that groups are fluid. Part of getting students ready to be engaged participants in responsive guided reading groups means explaining the purpose of guided reading. Even kindergarten and first-grade students can understand the idea of "just-right" books (Routman, 2002). Boushey and Moser (2006) use the analogy of shoe size, and they bring in a box of shoes at the beginning of the school year to make their point. In pulling out shoes of varying sizes, they demonstrate how some shoes are too big, some are too small, and some fit us just right. They compare this concept to the concept of "good-fit" books, demonstrating that some books are too easy, some are too hard, and some are just right for us. We like this analogy and think it's also helpful for explaining the need to have reading groups that sometimes change. We can ask students, "What happens when the shoes that fit you perfectly in July suddenly feel way too small in December?" They'll tell us that, of course, you would get new shoes. We can follow that up by asking, "What if the books that are just right for you in October suddenly seem too easy for you in November?" Students will see that it makes sense to read books that are a bit more challenging in that case. We explain that just as some kids' feet grow faster than others, so, too, do some kids show growth in reading at different rates, so that sometimes we will need to move kids from one group to another to make sure that they are still reading just-right books. If we make this very clear from the start, it will not seem strange to kids if they are moved into a different group during responsive guided reading. If we don't do this from the beginning, we find that kids get very used to the group that they're in and making changes in January or March may seem more jarring than if we are continually reevaluating and moving kids throughout the school year.

We do not need to do any formal or time-consuming assessments to make informed decisions about group placement in responsive guided reading. It's really pretty clear when students are not appropriately placed. Even our preservice teachers who work with a guided reading group can see right away if there are students who are reading above or below the level of the materials being used. Students for whom the material is too easy will not make any miscues at all, and their comprehension of materials will be good. Students for whom the material is too difficult will struggle throughout the selection. Their fluency will be poor, their attitudes may be negative, and their comprehension will certainly suffer. When we consider the purpose of responsive guided reading, we will remember that it is to listen to individual students read and to provide support to students as they make miscues. Chapters 4 and 5 provided specific suggestions for what this teacher support will look like, but clearly, if students can read all the words without errors and can easily comprehend the material, then we are not serving them well in a responsive guided reading group. For younger students, we would expect miscues about three to seven times for every 100 words, meaning that if we listen to a child read for about 2 minutes, and he or she reads about 30 WCPM, we can potentially provide decoding support for at least two words (taking into account how long it takes to help students with the miscued words). Students that don't miscue at all while they read or students who miscue more than 10 times per 100 words are reading materials that are inappropriate for them, and we will see that right away.

Teachers should take notes as they are listening to students read, recording what kinds of miscues they are making, what their affect is during reading, and if the material seems appropriate. We do suggest that teachers wait a day or two before making a move, just to see if their observations hold true during the next responsive guided reading group. After a teacher's observations are confirmed, the teacher should take the student aside and let that child know that the books he or she has been reading in responsive guided reading are no longer "good-fit" books and that the student is going to move to a different group. In the case where a child's reading has improved, it is perfectly appropriate to let the child know how well he or she is reading. In the case where a child is making a move into easier materials, it is also appropriate to let the student know why he or she is moving, making clear that just like wearing shoes that are too big is uncomfortable, so, too, is reading books that are too hard. A teacher can tell the child, too, that it may not be long before another move will need to be made. The more children see this happening with other students in the classroom, the less likely it is to seem punitive.

The following are two scenarios that demonstrate how Mrs. Bevington assesses children during responsive guided reading groups and makes changes as needed.

SCENARIO 1

Mrs. Bevington calls Charlie, Nicholas, Dorothy, Luke, and Evelyn over to the guided reading table. Today they are reading a book about a birthday party. The book is at Fountas and Pinnell (1996) level H. As Mrs. Bevington listens to each child read, she notices that Dorothy makes only one miscue while reading approximately 100 words and the miscue is an insertion of the word *the* before the phrase *birthday cake*. Mrs. Bevington writes the following on her clipboard: "Dorothy: only one miscue— insertion, didn't change meaning of text; comprehension excellent. Monitor miscues during next group—may need to move her into another group." The remaining group members read well but make enough miscues for Mrs. Bevington to be able to provide helpful scaffolding tailored to each child's individual challenges. The next time Mrs. Bevington meets with the group they are reading a book about the circus, which is still at Fountas and Pinnell level H. Again, Dorothy makes only one miscue, this time reading *elephants* as *elephant,* and again, she demonstrates good comprehension of what she's read. Mrs. Bevington takes Dorothy aside after the group is done and tells her, "Dorothy, you are reading so well that I'm beginning to think that these books may be too easy for you. Remember when we talked about 'just-right' books and

I brought in the shoes to demonstrate that, just as some shoes are too big, and some are too small, but some are just right, so, too, are some books just right? I don't think these books are just right anymore, and I think you need more of a challenge. I am going to try you in a new group next time to see if we can find the 'just-right' group for you. I'm so proud of your reading and how well you are doing!"

SCENARIO 2

Mrs. Bevington calls Francisca, Nathaniel, Peter, and Dianna to the guided reading table. This group has struggled a bit during the first couple months of school, but have lately made good progress, and they are currently reading a book about an octopus which is at Fountas and Pinnell level E. Mrs. Bevington notes on her clipboard that Francisca, Nathaniel, and Peter have made a lot of progress decoding consonant blends and short vowel words, but after listening to Dianna, she notes that Dianna still struggles with all but the most basic words. She got tripped up with the *fr* blend in *frog*, read *shell* as *sal*, and couldn't get beyond the initial /w/ sound in *water*, even though that word should have been easy to determine given the picture and context. The book itself contains only 42 words, and Dianna miscued on three of the first 20 words, clearly making this book at her frustration level. Mrs. Bevington will see how Dianna does during the next reading group, but is pretty certain that she will need to move into the lowest reading group. After the next meeting of this group, Mrs. Bevington feels that her observations about Dianna have been confirmed and she takes her aside to tell her about the move. "Dianna," she says, "tell me what you think about the books we have been reading. Do they feel like 'just-right' books to you?" Dianna shrugs and looks down. "I've noticed that some of the words seem pretty hard for you, would you agree?" Dianna nods. "That's okay, Dianna. That's nothing to be ashamed of. Remember, it is my job to find books that are 'just right' for you, and I don't think I've done a good job of that in this group. I am beginning to think that if you were to join Sam and Ella in their group, we may be able to find books that are 'just right' for you. Do you want to give it a try?" Dianna nods. "Good! Won't it feel great to read books that are just a little easier for you? Sam and Ella will be so happy to have you in their group!" Mrs. Bevington notices that when she works with Sam, Ella, and Dianna over time, Dianna seems more animated and much more confident than in her previous group.

OTHER KINDS OF GROUPING SCENARIOS IN CLASS

It has been our experience that no matter how flexible we make our responsive guided reading groups, no matter how we try to move kids around so that there is no sense of permanence in the groups, some kids still pick up on the differences between groups and get a sense of who the "high readers" and the "low readers" are. This is an unfortunate by-product of guided reading, and one that can be modified by making sure readers do not get "stuck" in the same group throughout the year or throughout their schooling. However, to combat this impression that students pick up on about high and low readers, we also believe in creating grouping opportunities throughout the literacy block that can incorporate our weaker and stronger readers, so that students of all abilities have opportunities to work together.

One way teachers can do this is through book discussion groups. A form of book discussion groups that we think works well with heterogeneous groups (and is a good precursor to literature circles) is one where the teacher reads aloud a great picture book, such as *Chicken Sunday* by Patricia Polacco, and then breaks the students into small groups to discuss the book. Because students don't have to do any reading themselves, it works very well to mix abilities in the discussion groups, where kids that may be perceived as the struggling readers have an opportunity to be successful in a situation where their ideas can be heard without having to approach text that may be challenging. Often teachers start this process in a whole group, where they pose questions about the text and model what a discussion of those questions might look like. After a lot of whole-group practice, teachers ultimately allow the students to participate in their own discussions, which they monitor by moving from one group to the next.

Literature circles are also an opportunity for students to read books together, based on their own interests rather than their reading ability. Books for literature circles often reflect a specific theme and teachers allow students to choose their top two to three choices for reading, irrespective of ability level. Teachers place students in groups based on their choices and also based on which children they think would work well together. Even if the books are beyond certain children's reading levels, this discrepancy can be accommodated by allowing some kids to listen to tape-recorded readings of the books or even read the books at home with a sibling or parent. The classroom portion of literature circles is the book discussion. Many models of literature circles allow for multiple strengths to emerge during these discussions. For example, one common literature circle role is the "illustrator" who is asked to create a drawing that best illustrates an important part of the book. This allows for someone who may be more graphically talented to shine, even if he or she is not a particularly strong reader.

Reader's Theatre performances are also an opportunity for students to work in heterogeneous groups. Most Reader's Theatre scripts, or indeed most picture books that can be used for Readers Theatre, have a variety of roles with greater or lesser difficulty. Students can work in a Readers Theatre group where some students will need to read comparatively more than others, and that allows for students of different abilities to work together to create a performance.

The more our students see that everyone in class has opportunities to work with each other, regardless of reading level, the less likely it is that kids will perceive themselves or others as the "high" or "low" students in class. They may begin to see, instead, that each of them brings unique strengths to their classroom interactions. For some, that may be a great vocabulary, for others that may be artistic strengths, and for still others that may be analytical abilities manifested in discussions.

Responsive guided reading groups should continue to be as homogeneous as possible so that teachers can best provide support to their students that is tailor-made just for them, using materials that are neither too difficult nor too easy. However, teachers help students to understand that one's reading ability at a particular point in time is not reflective of who that child will be as a reader 1 month or 1 year from now. Students should all have the opportunity to improve, to move from group to group, and to develop as readers at a pace that is comfortable for them.

RESOURCES FOR FURTHER READING

Boushey, G., & Moser, J. (2009). *The CAFE book: Engaging all students in daily literary assessment and instruction.* York, ME: Stenhouse.

This book provides many helpful examples of conferences between teachers and students, and explains how teachers can use those conferences to assess student needs and make decisions about grouping. The authors show how brief and targeted conferences can provide rich information about students' growth in reading as well as their areas of need. In addition, the appendix includes forms teachers can use when meeting with students in order to record essential information.

Caldwell, J. & Ford, M. P. (2002). *Where have all the bluebirds gone?: How to soar with flexible grouping.* Portsmouth, NH: Heinemann.

The authors aim to create a vision of classroom reading programs far different from that of past programs, which honored static ability grouping. They describe a variety of flexible grouping patterns and ways to implement them in elementary classrooms. Pros and cons of each are also discussed so teachers can make informed decisions and avoid common pitfalls. Helpful classroom snapshots at a variety of grade levels are also included.

Diller, D. (2007). *Making the most of small groups: Differentiation for all.* York, ME: Stenhouse.

This book focuses on the teacher's role during small-group instruction. There is a chapter devoted to grouping, which discusses how to ensure groups are flexible using formal and informal assessments, and carefully organizing and managing results. The author then devotes a chapter to each essential reading element: comprehension, fluency, phonemic awareness, phonics, and vocabulary. She presents numerous practical applications in each area by offering teacher promptings, possible lesson focuses, and even detailed lesson plans.

Opitz, M. F., & Ford, M. P. (2001). *Reaching readers: Flexible and innovative strategies for guided reading.* Portsmouth, NH: Heinemann.

The authors call their model a "second-generation" model of guided reading, one that challenges educators to expand their vision and experiment with alternative practices. The chapter devoted to grouping discusses grouping options, myths, and other frequently asked grouping questions. The appendix contains assessment procedures and protocol forms that will aid teachers in forming and reforming groups based on readers' skills and abilities to use strategies.

Chapter 10

Selecting Materials
for Responsive
Guided Reading Groups

"I'm supposed to teach guided reading,
but the only leveled readers we have
are from the publisher of our reading
series, and they're terrible!"

"Okay, I've divided my class into groups
according to their instructional needs. Now what
books am I supposed to give them to read?!"

Searching for and finding materials for guided reading groups is one of the most difficult parts of guided reading. Three issues come up frequently: First, it can be difficult for teachers to find appropriate materials for each of their guided reading groups. Second, even when they have access to leveled readers in their schools, teachers are not always satisfied with the quality of the materials. Third, many of the teachers we know feel compelled to match guided reading materials to the topics or themes they are covering during shared reading or even science or social studies, and they therefore spend excessive amounts of time searching for materials on a common theme. This chapter addresses these three issues.

FINDING APPROPRIATE GUIDED READING MATERIALS

We find that the teachers with whom we work struggle to select texts for guided reading groups because they are so eager for students to succeed that they choose books that aren't difficult enough. The beauty of the responsive guided reading group is that the student has the opportunity to confront difficult material with a supportive adult immediately available as a scaffold. If the text does not force the student to miscue quickly, this structure is not necessary and the time has not been productive. One of the most important things to remember about guided reading materials is that they should match the instructional reading level of the students in each group. In other words, the materials used should force kids to make errors 5–10% of the time. The learning opportunities afforded in responsive guided reading groups will not take place if the child does not make a miscue or otherwise demonstrate a reading breakdown. The following example illustrates a child and teacher working together on three different leveled texts. You will see the missed opportunities that arise from choosing a text that is either too easy or too difficult.

Example

Material That Is Too Easy

Jonathan, a second grader, reads aloud from Crockett Johnson's *A Picture for Harold's Room* while his teacher listens. This book is at a Fountas and Pinnell (1996) level H.

JONATHAN: I want a picture to put on my wall," says Harold. He drew a house with his purple crayon. More houses made a little ... t ... t ... town. It was far away. The town had woods and hills around it. And it was at the end of a long road. "It will look pretty in the moon ... l ... light," said Harold. And he stepped up into the picture to draw the moon. He looked down at the house ... I mean houses. "I am a GIANT!" he said. But a giant would scare all the people in town.

TEACHER: Wow, Jonathan. You read very well. There were a couple words that you didn't recognize at first, but you took your time and figured them out. Well done!

Words read correctly in 2 minutes: 90; miscues: 1, self-corrected; accuracy: 100% (independent level).

Material That Is Just Right

Jonathan reads aloud from Arnold Lobel's *Frog and Toad Together*, which is at Fountas and Pinnell level K.

JONATHAN: Frog was in his gar ... garage.

TEACHER: Garage? Look at the picture, does that look like a garage?

JONATHAN: No, it's a garden. Frog was in his garden.

TEACHER: Good ... remember, you can use the pictures to help you figure out words. Keep reading!

JONATHAN: Toad came walking by. "What a fine gar ... garden you have, Frog," he said. "Yes," said Frog. But it was had work."

TEACHER: Had work? Does that make sense? Why don't you read that again, and remember that it ought to make sense!

JONATHAN: Hard work.

TEACHER: Good!

JONATHAN: "I wish I had a garden," said Toad. "Here are some flower seeds. Put them in the ground," said Frog...

TEACHER: (*pointing to the word* plant) What did you say this word was?

JONATHAN: *Put.*

TEACHER: I think there's a little word in this word that you know. Let's cover up the *pl.* Do you know this word?

JONATHAN: *Ant.*

TEACHER: That's right! Now let's uncover these letters and let you try it again.

JONATHAN: P ... l ... ant. Plant!

TEACHER: That's right!

JONATHAN: "Plant them in the ground," said Frog.

TEACHER: Great reading, Jonathan! You used many different strategies to figure out words you were unsure of!

Words read correctly in 2 minutes: 51; miscues: 3; accuracy: 94% (instructional level).

Material That Is Too Difficult

Jonathan reads aloud from Kate Waters's *Fires and Floods,* which is at Fountas and Pinnell level M.

JONATHAN: Fire and water are im … im … interesting?

TEACHER: Interesting is a good guess, because it makes sense and begins with *i.* Let's look at that word again. It's a big word. Let's try to read the different parts of it. You already know it begins with *im.* Let's cover up the beginning and end of the word. What do you see?

JONATHAN: *Port?*

TEACHER: That's right. Now let's look just at the end of the word. (*Covers up all but* ant.)

JONATHAN: *Ant?*

TEACHER: That's right. Now let's put all those parts together. *Im … port … ant.*

JONATHAN: *Im … port … ant?* I don't know what that word is.

TEACHER: That's okay. You gave it a great try. The word is *important.* Point to the word and say *important.* Now keep reading.

JONATHAN: They can help us. But they can hurt us, too. Fire gives us … liget?

TEACHER: Does that make sense? Let's look at the word. Are these letters [*ight*] in any of our words on the word wall.

JONATHAN: (*looking at the word wall*) *Right?*

TEACHER: Yes, now take off the *r* and put the *l* at the beginning instead.

JONATHAN: *Light?* Fire gives us light so we can see. It wams us up. Woms us up. (*Looks to teacher.*)

TEACHER: That doesn't make sense, does it? What can fire help us do when we're cold? Get w …

JONATHAN: Warm!

TEACHER: Yes, that's right!

Words read correctly in 2 minutes: 27; miscues: 3; accuracy: 88% (frustration level).

The three scenarios described above show how important using appropriate materials is for the success of responsive guided reading groups.

In the first scenario, Jonathan has no difficulty reading the passage. He hesitates in spots, and misreads and self-corrects the word *houses.* However, the teacher doesn't need to provide any support while he reads. This is clearly a book that Jonathan could be reading independently.

The second scenario shows Jonathan reading text that is just right for responsive guided reading. He only reads for 2 minutes, but makes three miscues that allow the teacher to go over some important decoding strategies. With her prompts, he quickly decodes the words and moves on. He is able to read 51 words correctly in 2 minutes, including time spent interacting with the teacher. We say this text is instructional for Jonathan.

Finally, in the third scenario, Jonathan gets tripped up three times within the first 27 words of the passage. The teacher spends so much time providing support that Jonathan reads very few words and loses the meaning of the text, meaning this book is at his frustration level.

So, how do you find materials that will appropriately challenge students? Most schools or school districts purchase a basal series from an educational publisher, and often guided reading materials are included with the series. Many schools also supplement these publisher-provided materials with sets of leveled books purchased from another source. The net result is that we have found most teachers have access to many materials appropriate for responsive guided reading. (We will discuss below what teachers can do when they do not have access to leveled books.) Some teachers are even lucky enough to work in schools where they have access to a book room, where books are arranged by reading level, and all teachers have to do is find books at the instructional level of each of their groups in class.

Deciphering Reading Levels

Books are leveled based on certain criteria, including number of words per selection, words per page, number of different words, number of high- and low-frequency words, sentence length, sentence complexity, illustration support, and so on. While all books are leveled using these criteria, there are multiple leveling systems that vary depending on which reading series a teacher accesses. Some schools use the Reading Recovery leveling system, which uses a numbering system, ranging from 1 (in kindergarten) to 34 (in eighth grade) to indicate different reading levels. Schools that rely on the Diagnostic Reading Assessment (DRA) will also use numbers to level books, but with a slightly different system (ranging from 1 in kindergarten to 44 in fifth grade) than the Reading Recovery system. The schools that use Fountas and Pinnell materials will use alphabet letters to indicate different levels (A is at the beginning of kindergarten and Z at eighth grade), while many schools have started to use lexiles to indicate instructional levels, which are indicated by numbers ranging from 200 (at first grade) to 1,100 (at eighth grade). Other schools rely on grade-level equivalents, while still other schools may have a self-created leveling system to incorporate all the different kinds of readers they have purchased.

What further complicates things is that some schools have leveled books that represent more than one of the leveling systems described above, so at any one time a first-grade teacher may be using a Reading Recovery level-2 book with her lowest group, a Fountas and Pinnell level-C book with her next group, a DRA level-8 book with another group, and a book with the lexile of 250 for her top group. Refer to Figure 10.1 to see the different leveling systems and how they correspond with one another. We hope this figure will be a useful reference as you begin to make sense of leveled books and students' instructional levels.

Though reading levels do give teachers a means for determining material appropriateness for guided reading groups, they can be somewhat confusing. These leveling systems are always a good place to start, but nothing replaces listening to a student read to determine if the level is correct. We think one of the most important things to remember is that materials used during responsive guided reading should be challenging enough to students to force them to miscue about five to 10 times per 100 words. This may mean a teacher needs to do a bit of detective work as responsive guided reading gets off the ground in her classroom in order to find the most appropriate materials. We have seen teachers use books that were a good deal more difficult than the assessments determined her students would be able to read, yet students were able to read them. Rather than cling to levels that are indicated by assessments, teachers should judge whether a book will do what it needs to do for students to make quick and clear errors that can become fodder for instruction.

Let's use the example of guided reading groups in a third-grade classroom from Chapter 8 (see page 119), so that we can consider what a teacher would need to do to find appropriate materials for each group. Some teachers will use instinct far more than formula to make determinations about appropriate books. Others will rely upon a building reading specialist or literacy coach to assist with this process. These literacy professionals are highly trained in assessments and interpretations of those assessments and can be a valuable resource. We think teachers should at least know how to gather and use this information, so we have provided an example below. Though it gets technical at

Grade level	Reading recovery	Fountas–Pinnell guided reading	DRA	Basal equivilant	Lexile levels
Kindergarten	A, B	A	A	Readiness	
	1		1	Readiness	
	2	B	2	PrePrimer 1	
	3	C	3	PrePrimer 1	
	4	C	4		
Grade 1	5	D	6	PrePrimer 2	
	6	D		PrePrimer 3	
	7	E	8	PrePrimer 3	
	8	E			
	9	F	10	Primer	
	10	F		Primer	
	11	G	12		
	12	G			
	13	H	14	Grade 1	200–299
	14	H		Grade 1	
	15	I	16		
	16	I			
Grade 2	18	J, K	20	Grade 2	300–399
	20	L, M	28		400–499
Grade 3	22	N	30	Grade 3	500–599
		N	34	Grade 3	
	24	O, P	38		600–699
Grade 4	26	Q, R, S	40	Grade 4	700–799
Grade 5	28	T, U, V	44	Grade 5	800–899
Grade 6	30	W, X, Y		Grade 6	900–999
Grade 7	32	Z		Grade 7	1000–1100
Grade 8	34	Z		Grade 8	1000–1100

FIGURE 10.1. Reading level correlation chart. Reprinted by permission of West Bloomfield Township Public Library.

times, we think even a quick read-through can provide teachers with good background knowledge of this assessment and selection process. For further reading on this process, please refer to Fountas and Pinnell (1996) who give a helpful overview of assessing and selecting appropriate materials. If the level of detail provided below becomes daunting for you as a new teacher or a teacher new to these practices, skip ahead to the section called "What If I Don't Have Access to Leveled Materials?" You know that this example is here, and you can always return to it at a later time.

A Third-Grade Teacher Determines Which Materials Are Appropriate for Her Responsive Guided Reading Groups

During the first month of school the third-grade teacher had determined that two of her students were well below average in their reading fluency, and their accuracy on third-grade reading materials (as ascertained by a fluency snapshot) was well below 90%. The teacher knew that these students were not reading at the third-grade level, but she didn't know at exactly what level they were. If she had time in that first month to do a running record with these students, she would have been able to pinpoint much more precisely at which level the students were; however, in this case, the teacher was unfamiliar with running records and so, come October (and the beginning of responsive guided reading), she only knew that they were struggling and well below the level of most other students in class. Our recommendation to her would be to seek out copies of books at different levels (perhaps Reading Recovery levels 14, 15, and 16) to bring to her first meeting with this guided reading group. Starting with the easiest of the three books (level 14), she could simply listen to each of the two students read for 2–3 minutes to determine the level appropriateness. Jotting down the miscues that each student made, the teacher could then determine the number of words the students could read correctly, and divide that by the number of words that they read in total, to determine the percentage accuracy. The formula for determining accuracy is as follows:

Number of words read correctly ÷ total words read = percentage accuracy

Student 1 read 90 words in 2 minutes (her fluency was slightly higher than it was for her fluency snapshot, as she was reading first-grade materials). She miscued on three of those words. We determine that she read 87 words correctly, and following the formula just described, we divide those 87 words by the 90 total words that she read, and come up with an accuracy percentage of 96.7. This means that she is *independent* at Reading Recovery level 14. Similarly, we find that Student 2 reads with almost 98% accuracy at level 14. The teacher next does the same thing with the Reading Recovery level-15 book. This time she determines that while the students are less fluent with this passage, they nevertheless are reading with 91% and 94% accuracy, respectively.

Though for both students, this *is* instructional, it is wise for the teacher to see how the students do with the level-16 book, because it is better for the students to be reading books that are slightly too hard than to read books that are slightly too easy during responsive guided reading. This time, she finds that one student is reading the level-16 book with almost 88% accuracy, and the other is reading with slightly higher than 90% accuracy. She determines that level-15 books, which were at both students' instructional level (and represent the end of first-grade reading level), will be most appropriate for this group, and will select one such book to use when she meets with this group next. Given how close the level-16 books were to being instructional for these students, however, she knows that these students will likely move up a level soon and that she should continue to assess during each guided reading group to make sure that they are appropriately challenged.

With her second group, the teacher recalls that the three students read a third-grade passage with below-average fluency and with 85–90% accuracy. This means that third-grade materials are at their frustration level, but only barely. Looking at the guided reading materials, she decides to select a book at level 18 and another at level 20 (second-grade-level books) to try out with the students during their first guided reading meeting. She finds that the level-18 book is at the independent level of two of the three students (96% and 98% accuracy, respectively). The third student reads the level-18 passage with 94% accuracy, which means the passage is instructional for that student. The teacher decides to see how each of the students does with the level-20 book. The first student reads 134 out of 145 words accurately, an accuracy percentage of 92%. The second student reads 136 out of 150 words accurately, an accuracy percentage of 90.6%. The third student struggled somewhat more than the two students above, reading 107 out of 120 words accurately. His percentage accuracy of 89% indicates that this book is at his frustration level. The teacher considers placing the student in the lowest group, but decides to see how the student does with level-20 books over the next few guided reading lessons.

With her third group, the teacher has already determined that the six students within the group are reading at about the third-grade level, based on their performance on the fluency snapshots. She decides that she will start them in level-22 materials, which are considered to be beginning of third-grade level, but she will be alert to student performance during guided reading in order to determine if level 22 is too difficult or too easy for some of the students. Similarly, she decides to start her fourth group in level-24 materials, which are end of third-grade level, because these students performed slightly above average on the fluency snapshots she administered in September. Again, she will be paying close attention to the seven students in this group to determine if they are being appropriately challenged by level-24 materials.

Finally, the teacher brings several different sets of books to her first meeting with her fifth group, who were all clearly above grade level based on their performance on the fluency snapshots. She first has them read from the level-24 selection, though she is not surprised that each of the six students in the group read it with above 95% accuracy. The table below shows how the students performed on subsequent reading selections.

	Student 1	Student 2	Student 3	Student 4	Student 5	Student 6
Level 24	98%	96%	99%	98%	96%	97%
Level 26	95%	92%	96%	94%	90%	94%
Level 28	92%	90%	93%	90%	88%	92%

The teacher is unsure what to do about choosing an appropriate reading level for this group. On the one hand, all but Student 3 is instructional at level 26. But then again, all but Student 5 are instructional at level 28. She decides to start with level-28 materials, since they are most appropriate for five of the six students, knowing that she will need to keep an eye on Student 5. If she perceives that Student 5 is far too frustrated during guided reading group, making so many miscues that comprehension of the materials is compromised, then she may decide to move Student 5 into another group.

What If I Don't Have Access to Leveled Materials?

While we have found that most teachers we work with do have access to an ample supply of leveled materials for guided reading, there are schools that do not have enough suitable materials. In fact, it is not uncommon for schools to require teachers to do guided reading while telling them that they must use the grade-level materials provided (e.g., basal readers). Anyone with an idea of what guided reading is would understand that you cannot use grade-level materials if you have students reading below or above grade level, so it is helpful if teachers have some ideas about what to do if this is the case.

Pool Your Resources

We recommend that you work with other classroom teachers in your school to pool your resources. If you are a second-grade teacher and have a classroom supply of second-grade basal readers and perhaps multiple copies of second-grade-level trade books, then you should talk with the first- and third-grade teachers at your school to see if they would be willing to share their resources with you as well. Together, you may have access to first- through third-grade-appropriate texts, which would go a long way toward helping you provide differentiated materials to the different students in your class. You can help other teachers see the value in this approach by explaining that they will surely have students reading above or below grade level themselves, and having access to second-grade materials would expand their resources as well. The more teachers you can encourage to pool their resources, the better. It is helpful if you can create a catalog of resources available so that every teacher knows what he or she can choose from. Even if the only reading materials you have are basal readers, at least you know that you can use a first-grade-level basal with your struggling second graders if necessary, in order to better meet their needs and challenges. Teachers should not worry that material will be repeated in future grades. Students' literacy will move along, and thus the books that they use this year will not be at their instructional level next year. We often hear the concern that advanced students, reading at materials several grade levels above, will repeat this material later. This should not be the case if all teachers are using differentiated instruction. Even if the student does see something again because a teacher has not differentiated in this same manner, it will be fine. Students often welcome, or fail to notice, rereading materials.

Many teachers also subscribe to periodicals like *Scholastic News* or *Weekly Reader*. Though teachers tend to use these in a whole-class setting, they could also be used for guided reading materials. Imagine if, as a second-grade teacher, you could use the second-grade *Scholastic News* during guided reading with your average readers, but you also had access to the first- and third-grade versions to use with your below- and above-average readers. Your students would all be getting the same news but at levels that each found accessible and appropriately challenging.

Utilize Online Resources

Do an online search of "news for kids" and you'd be amazed at all the Internet sites that are designed for children. The above-mentioned

Scholastic News and *Weekly Reader* each have online sites, as does *Time for Kids* and *National Geographic Kids*. Beyond that, many of the big news operations for adults also offer content for children. Most of these sites are also accessible for free. Some of them even offer "leveled" options so that you can, for example, read a story on *Time for Kids* about outer space that is written for K–1, 2–3, or 4–6. To be sure, this online content isn't as finely leveled as the guided reading materials available to some teachers, but it at least offers options that are engaging to children, and somewhat differentiated as well. In addition, many of the online sites for kids offer related materials, teaching tips, and ideas for projects and story extensions. One of the advantages of using these resources is that they offer our students guided practice in nonfiction materials that are of high interest to students, something that is often missing in our fiction-centered classrooms.

In addition to online news sources for kids, there are many, many options for finding online leveled books. Do an online search of "leveled readers" and you'll find many websites offering free leveled readers, particularly for emerging readers, that you can print out for use in guided reading. There are also websites such as *ReadingAtoZ.com* which offer, for a fee, unlimited guided readers for all levels of students. If your school lacks guided reading materials, it may be worth it to have access to such a site.

Expand Your Own Classroom Library

Teachers are well known for spending their own money on resources for their classroom, and though we are loathe to encourage this practice, we do understand that there is often no alternative. That being said, it is important to consider how teachers can purchase reasonably priced materials that will assist them in guided reading.

Many teachers send home monthly book orders so that their students can order books at reasonable prices to read at home. Teachers should be aware that not only are books often offered at bargain prices, but such book orders typically provide teachers with points for every dollar spent by students. These points can be used to purchase gift-type items, but they can also be used to purchase multiple copies of books, which are often offered at discount prices already. Shipping on book orders tends to be free.

Savvy teachers have also been known to utilize eBay or similar Internet sites in order to purchase sets of guided readers which are frequently offered at very low prices by teachers who are retiring or changing grades.

Finally, some teachers who have enough scented candles and apple-shaped pins to last a lifetime ask parents who wish to honor them during holidays or on teacher appreciation day to purchase books or gift cards that can be used by the teacher to purchase classroom books.

Once you have obtained multiple copies of books at different grade levels, it is helpful to ascertain what the reading level of each book is. There are data banks of leveled books at several different online sites including one at the Scholastic website called *bookwizard.scholastic.com*. At this site you are directed to enter the name of a book, and the web site will tell you what reading level that book is (including grade-level equivalent, DRA system, Fountas and Pinnell system, or lexile). This is helpful because often grade levels that are provided by publishers offer a range of grades (e.g., K–2) that isn't nearly specific enough for responsive guided reading purposes. It may be helpful to determine the reading level of books in your classroom library as well, so that you can help students pick appropriate books for independent reading. Another benefit of the Teacher Book Wizard website is that you can enter a specific reading level (as well as other information including topic, genre, etc.) and the site will give you a list of books that are at that reading level. This can be very useful as you make decisions about which books would be most beneficial for your specific grade level and students.

IT'S OKAY IF YOU (AND YOUR STUDENTS) DON'T LOVE YOUR GUIDED READING MATERIALS

Some teachers have access to multiple leveled books for guided reading and do not have to scramble just to find materials. However, one complaint we often hear is that teachers are discouraged by the quality of the titles they have at their disposal for guided reading. We acknowledge that this can be a challenge, and indeed we have seen some books that seem to have very little literary merit. While we do not encourage schools to purchase materials that are anything other than excellent, we must acknowledge that weaker materials are often available as readily as are good materials, and often teachers must use materials that they have at the ready.

In responsive guided reading, the goal is learning how to read beyond the text at hand. The text thus becomes a tool for learning a new strategy rather than an end unto itself. Children can surely understand that sometimes the materials we read are useful because they teach something about reading. Sometimes the materials we read fascinate us and our students, but not always. Some guided reading books are helpful because they illustrate a certain point related to reading, or are ideal for practicing a particular strategy. We sometimes talk to students about the difference between reading and practicing reading. We read to gain information, for pleasure, or to understand our worlds better. Good books help us to do that. We practice reading to get better at reading for pleasure, to gain information, or to learn about the world. Good and not-so-good books can help us with this. While we would always select a higher quality book over a lower quality book when given the choice, we ask teachers not to work so hard to find engaging books that they run out of steam for conducting responsive guided reading.

Similarly, we know teachers who believe that the literacy block should be linked by a common theme. Consider a teacher that is doing a unit on fairy tales, a common unit for the primary grades. She has fairy tales in big book form to read during shared reading, beautiful multicultural fairy tales to read during the read-aloud, and she finds dozens of fairy tales in her own collection and from the library for students to read during independent reading. Often this same teacher spends an inordinate time finding multiple copies of fairy tales, at the different reading levels of her different guided reading groups, to read during responsive guided reading. While we do believe this is a marvelous way to unite the literacy block, we also feel strongly that matching guided reading materials to the theme being explored in the rest of reading and language arts is unnecessarily taxing and time-consuming, particularly for the teacher who is new to guided reading. There are enough pieces to put into place—assessing and grouping students according to their instructional level, training the students to work in small groups and independently, and also planning the activities for the rest of the class. On top of this, to ask teachers to find books on the same theme, when their guided reading selections may be limited at best, is to promote a seriously misguided expenditure of time.

For teachers just getting started with responsive guided reading, the most important criteria for choosing books is that they match the instructional needs of their students. That means we do spend time determining reading levels and understanding which students need which level of books. And while we attempt to find the best possible selections, if we find that guided reading materials are not as exhilarating or engaging as we would hope, it is okay. The most important aspect of responsive guided reading is finding materials that are just challenging enough so that when we listen to a child read, he or she will make mistakes and we can help that child come up with a strategy or strategies for correcting those mistakes. This should remain our focus.

RESOURCES FOR FURTHER READING

Fountas, I. C., & Pinnell, G. S. (2005). *Leveled books K–8: Matching texts to readers for effective teaching.* Portsmouth, NH: Heinemann.

This book will help teachers understand how to use leveled books in their classrooms. The leveling process is explained in detail, and characteristics for books at each level are described. Teachers will be informed on how to select books, use benchmark books, and create an effective classroom library.

Fountas, I. C., & Pinnell, G. S. (2009). *The Fountas and Pinnell leveled book list, K–8.* Portsmouth, NH: Heinemann.

This comprehensive list includes 18,000 book titles, leveled A through Z (K–8) by the authors. The first half of the book presents the books alphabetically by title; the second half is organized by book level. This is a great resource for teachers to use when matching books to readers.

Szymusiak, K., Sibberson, F., & Koch, L. (2008). *Beyond leveled books: Supporting early and transitional readers in grades K–5* (2nd ed.). York, ME: Stenhouse.

This book offers instructional tools, ideas, and book titles that will guide transitional readers into independence. The authors enable educators to look beyond book levels and recognize the supports that different texts offer readers such as organization, text layout, and dialogue.

References

Allen, J. (2000). *Yellow brick roads: Shared and guided paths to independent reading 4–12.* Portland, ME: Stenhouse.

Allington, R., & Cunningham, P. (2006). *Schools that work: Where all children read and write.* Boston: Allyn & Bacon.

Anderson, R. C., Hiebert, E. H., Scott, J. A., & Wilkinson, I. A. (1985). *Becoming a nation of readers: The report of the Commission on Reading.* Champaign–Urbana, IL: Center for the Study of Reading.

Atwell, N. (1998). *In the middle: New understandings about writing, reading, and learning.* Portsmouth, NH: Boynton-Cook.

Beers, K. (2002). *When kids can't read, what teachers can do: A guide for teachers 6–12.* Portsmouth, NH: Heinemann.

Blachowicz, C., & Fisher, P. J. (2009). *Teaching vocabulary in all classrooms* (4th ed.). Boston: Allyn & Bacon.

Blachowicz, C., & Ogle, D. (2008). *Reading comprehension: Strategies for independent learners* (2nd ed.). New York: Guilford Press.

Blachowicz, C. L. Z., Sullivan, D. M., & Cieply, C. (2001). Fluency snapshots: A quick screening tool for your classroom. *Reading Psychology, 22,* 95–109.

Block, C. C., & Paris, S. R. (Eds.). (2008). *Comprehension instruction: Research-based best practices* (2nd ed.). New York: Guilford Press.

Boushey, G., & Moser, J. (2006). *The daily 5: Fostering literacy independence in the elementary grades.* York, ME: Stenhouse.

Clay, M. M. (2000). *Running records: For classroom teachers.* Portsmouth, NH: Heinemann.

Clay, M. M. (2001). *Change over time in children's literacy development.* Portsmouth, NH: Heinemann.

Clay, M. M. (2006). *An observation survey of early literacy achievement: Revised second edition.* Portsmouth, NH: Heinemann.

Cole, A. D. (2006). Scaffolding beginning readers: Micro and macro cues teachers use during student oral reading. *Reading Teacher, 59*, 450–459.

Cunningham, P. M., & Allington, R. L. (2007). *Classrooms that work: They can all read and write* (4th ed.). Boston: Allyn & Bacon.

Cunningham, P. M., & Hall, D. P. (2001). *Making words second grade: 100 hands-on lessons for phonemic awareness, phonics, and spelling.* Grand Rapids, MI: Schaffer.

Cunningham, P. M., Hall, D. P., & Cunningham, J. W. (2000). *Guided reading the four-blocks way: The four-blocks literacy model book series.* Greensboro, NC: Carson-Dellosa.

Cunningham, P. M., Hall, D. P., & Heggie, T. (2001). *Making words.* Grand Rapids, MI: Schaffer.

Cunningham, P. M., Hall, D. P., & Sigmon, C. M. (2000). *The teachers' guide to the four blocks: A multimethod, multilevel framework for grades 1–3.* Greensboro, NC: Carson-Dellosa.

Diller, D. (2003). *Literacy work stations: Making centers work.* York, ME: Stenhouse.

Diller, D. (2005). *Practice with purpose: Literacy work stations for grades 3–6.* York, ME: Stenhouse.

Dorn, L. , French, C., & Jones, T. (1998). *Apprenticeship in learning: Transitions across reading and writing.* Portland, ME: Stenhouse.

Duffy, G. (1997). Powerful models or powerful teachers?: An argument for teacher-as-entrepreneur. In S. A. Stahl & D. A. Hayes (Eds.), *Instructional models in reading* (pp. 351–365). Mahwah, NJ: Erlbaum.

Duke, N., & Pearson, P. D. (2002). Effective practices for developing reading comprehension. In A. E. Farstrup & S. J. Samuels (Eds.), *What research has to say about reading instruction* (3rd ed., pp. 205–242). Newark, DE: International Reading Association.

Ford, M. P., & Opitz, M. F. (2008). Guided reading: Then and now. In M. J. Fresch (Ed.), *An essential history of current reading practices* (pp. 66–81). Newark, DE: International Reading Association.

Fountas, I. C., & Pinnell, G. S. (1996). *Guided reading: Good first teaching for all children.* Portsmouth, NH: Heinemann.

Graesser, A. C., McNamara, D. S., & Louwerse, M. M. (2003). What do readers need to learn in order to process coherence relations in narrative and expository text? In A. P. Sweet & C. E. Snow (Eds.), *Rethinking reading comprehension* (pp. 82–98). New York: Guilford Press.

Harvey, S., & Goudvis, A. (2000). *Strategies that work: Teaching comprehension to enhance understanding.* Portland, ME: Stenhouse.

Harvey, S., & Goudvis, A. (2007). *Strategies that work: Teaching comprehension to enhance understanding* (2nd ed.). Portland, ME: Stenhouse.

Keene, E. O., & Zimmerman, S. (2007). *Mosaic of thought: The power of comprehension strategy instruction* (2nd ed.). Portsmouth, NH: Heinemann.

Kuhn, M., & Stahl, S. (1998). Teaching children to learn word meanings from context: A synthesis and some questions. *Journal of Literacy Research, 30*, 119–138.

Lesesne, T. S. (2003). *Making the match: The right book for the right reader at the right time, grades 4–12.* Portland, ME: Stenhouse.

Lortie, D. (1975). *Schoolteacher: A sociological study.* London: University of Chicago Press.

National Institute of Child Health and Human Development. (2000). *Report of the National Reading Panel. Teaching children to read: An evidence-based assessment of the scientific research literature on reading and its implications for reading instruction* (NIH Publication No. 00-4769). Washington, DC: U.S. Government Printing Office.

Opitz, M. F., & Ford, M. P. (2001). *Reaching readers: Flexible and innovative strategies for guided reading.* Portsmouth, NH: Heinemann.

Picard, S. (2005). Collaborative conversations about second-grade readers. *Reading Teacher, 58*, 458–464.

Pressley, M. (2000). What should comprehension instruction be the instruction of? In M. L. Kamil, P. Mosenthal, P. D. Pearson, & R. Barr (Eds.), *Handbook of reading research* (Vol. 3, pp. 545–560). Mahwah, NJ: Erlbaum.

RAND Reading Study Group. (2002). *Reading for understanding: Toward an R&D program in reading comprehension.* Retrieved October 14, 2009, from *www.rand.org/multi/achievementforall/reading/readreport.html.*

Rasinski, T. V. (2003). *The fluent reader: Oral reading strategies for building word recognition, fluency, and comprehension.* New York: Scholastic.

Routman, R. (2002). *Reading essentials.* Portsmouth, NH: Heinemann.

Schwarz, R. M. (2005). Decisions, decisions: Responding to primary students during guided reading. *Reading Teacher, 58*, 436–443.

Stahl, S. A., & Nagy, W. E. (2006). *Teaching word meanings.* Mahwah, NJ: Erlbaum.

Taylor, B. M., Peterson, D. P., Pearson, P. D., & Rodriguez, M. C. (2002). Looking inside classrooms: Reflecting on the "how" as well as the "what" in effective reading instruction. *Reading Teacher, 56*, 270–279.

Tompkins, G. (2009). *Literacy for the 21st century: A balanced approach* (5th ed.). Upper Saddle River, NJ: Prentice Hall.

Williams, J. (2002). Reading comprehension strategies and teacher preparation. In A. E. Farstrup & S. J. Samuels (Eds.), *What research has to say about reading instruction* (3rd ed., pp. 243–260). Newark, DE: International Reading Association.

Index

Page numbers followed by *f* indicate figure; *t* indicate table

Accuracy. *See* Miscue rate; Words
  correct per minute (WCPM)
Affect, in response to reading, 113,
  130–131
"After-reading" activities, 36–37
ai pattern, teaching approach, 17, 18*f*
Alliteration, for kindergartners, 115
Alphabet letter recognition, assessment
  of, 115
Alphabetic knowledge, teachers'
  observations of, 114
Anchor charts, 90
Assessment
  for group placement. *See* Group
    placement
  of independent literacy activities,
    105, 107, 109
  questions for. *See* Questioning
    strategies
  through shared reading, 19–
    20
  See also Fluency snapshots; Running
    records; Teacher observations
Assessment tests, for kindergartners,
  115
Attending cues, 69–71, 69*f*

Balanced literacy block
  additional resources for, 30–31
  areas of, 17
  components of, 18–24
  daily, weekly, and monthly planning
    for, 29*f*

independent literacy activities in,
  22–23
integrating activities of, 24–30
in kindergarten, example of, 24–26
read-alouds in, 20–21
release of responsibility in, 28, 30
responsive guided reading in, 21–22
role of responsive guided reading in,
  16–31
shared reading in, 18–20
teacher demonstrations and, 17
in third grade, 27
word study in, 23–24
writing instruction in, 24
Bargain for Frances, A (Hoban), 5
Beginning readers
  decoding emphasis and, 60
  teacher cues for, 45–58. *See also*
    Teacher cueing, for beginning
    readers
  See also Kindergarten; Lower grades
Big word strategy, 40
Body language, comprehension
  assessment and, 67
Book discussion groups, heterogeneous
  levels in, 133
Book selection, 136–150
  additional resources for, 150
  appropriate, 137–148
  criteria for, 9
  by English language learners, 84
  enjoyability concept and, 83–84
  for forcing miscueing, 38

155

Fiction texts
  assessing comprehension of, 67
  questions for assessing
    comprehension of, 68f
Fires and Floods (Waters), 138–140
First grade
  group changes in, scenario for,
    127–128
  group placement in, 116–120
  literacy-related science instruction in,
    15, 103, 104f
  read-alouds in, 21
  shared reading in, 19
Fluency, comprehension and, 63–64
Fluency snapshots
  and changing group placement, 125
  procedure for, 117–118
  third-grade grouping based on, 118,
    119f, 120
Fluent readers
  defined, 60
  teacher cueing for, 59–75. *See also*
    Teacher cueing, for fluent readers
    additional resources for, 74–75
Forcing miscues, 91–92
  book selection for, 38, 137
  for providing teaching guidelines, 8
  rationale for, 10
  text selection and, 6, 7–8
Fountas and Pinnell criteria, 140–141
Free reading, 22
Frog and Toad Together (Lobel), 138
Frustration-level texts, 9, 10, 62, 129,
    132, 139, 140, 144

Graphophonic cues, 49
Group placement, 112–122
  additional resources for, 121–122
  approaches to, 7t
  changing
    based on student needs versus
      abilities, 124
    dealing with stigma of, 133
    explaining to student, 126
    resources for, 134–135
    responsive guided reading and,
      124–125
    revisiting decisions and, 125–129
    revisiting on as-needed basis,
      129–132
    scenarios of, 131–132

  creativity in, 128–129
  flexible, 123–135, 131–132
  getting started with, 120–121
  for heterogeneous readers, 133
  informal assessment for, 130
  kinds of, 133–134
  and options to reading, 133–134
  reading assessments for
    in first grade and beyond, 116–120
    in kindergarten, 115–116
  teacher observations and, 112–114
  versus tracking, 123
*Growing up in Pioneer America: 1800–
    1890* (Josephson), 28
Guided reading, 17
  implementation difficulties, 3–4
  need for, 3
  versus responsive guided reading,
    5–6
  streamlining, 12. *See also* Responsive
    guided reading
  time constraints for, 4
  See also Responsive guided reading

If You Traveled West in a Covered Wagon
    (Levine), 105
Inattention, cueing for, 69–71, 69f
Independent literacy activities
  in classrooms, 103, 104f, 105
  combining with guided reading
    activities, 92–93
  differentiation of, 97–98
  in kindergarten, 24, 26
  literacy centers versus, 88t
  management and assessment of, 105,
    107, 109
  preparing children for, 88, 90
  scheduling, 86, 87f, 88, 89f
  selection and promotion of, 86, 87f, 88
  working with words, 101–103, 102t
Independent literacy work time
  defined, 80
  establishing routines for, 81
Independent reading, 17
  approaches to, 23
  book selection for, 83–84
  building capacity for, 83–84
  consistent exposure to, 99
  purposes of, 98
  roles in balanced literacy block, 22–23
  for third grade, 27